Introduction

This is a book of reminiscences by an old-time cowboy, in which I play the part of ghost writer. For a long time I have been interested in the history of the West, especially Wyoming and Montana, and I have put in what time I could out there, as well as in eastern libraries, digging among the records of the past. It was more or less inevitable that I should meet Mr. Abbott, who was one of Montana's best-known old-timers, and I did meet him in the summer of 1937. Having heard that he knew a lot of Montana history because he had lived it, I went out to see him on his ranch outside of Lewistown.

That first afternoon we got in my car and drove out to look at the holes in the ground which used to be Fort Maginnis, once an army post established for protection against raiding Blackfeet, now just another quiet spot in the midst of the hills. We wandered around the leveled site of the old post, picking up old nails and bits of broken glass empurpled by the sun of fifty years, and as we wandered we talked, about cowboys, and their girls good and bad, and his Indian mother-in-law, and the work of Granville Stuart's raiders. For E. C. Abbott was a cowboy himself in the great days of the seventies and eighties; he came up the trail from Texas with the long-horned herds which stocked the northern ranges; he punched cows in Montana when there wasn't a fence in the territory; he married a daughter of Granville Stuart, great early-day stockman and outstanding Montana pioneer. For the past fifty-some years he has been known to cowmen from Texas to Alberta as Teddy "Blue," a nickname which has a story behind it, duly told in the following pages.

When I left him in August, 1937, he and Mrs. Abbott invited me to come back and spend a few days with them some time, and talk some more. That winter I accepted their invitation. I had been doing some rather extensive research for a novel about the old cowpunching West. I went back to Mr. Abbott to get background for my book and I found out that he had a book of his own. This discovery dawned gradually, in the course of five of the most exciting days I have ever spent. From taking notes in the ordinary way, which I soon found wouldn't do at all, a method grew of itself until, in the end, I was practically taking dictation from him—which was difficult because I don't know shorthand. Naturally those five days were only the beginning of our collaboration; I went back for other visits later, to finish up.

In his rush and drive to tell his story it came out helter-skelter, all over place and time—from Texas to Montana to Nebraska and from 1871 to 1889. But afterwards, when I fitted the pieces together, they dovetailed with never a hairbreadth inconsistency in dates or facts. Within my own limited knowledge I never found him in error. I interrupted him continually with questions: "When was that?" "Where were you?" "What did he look like?" Again and again I made him tell a story over two and three times before I had the details and the language right—and it would come

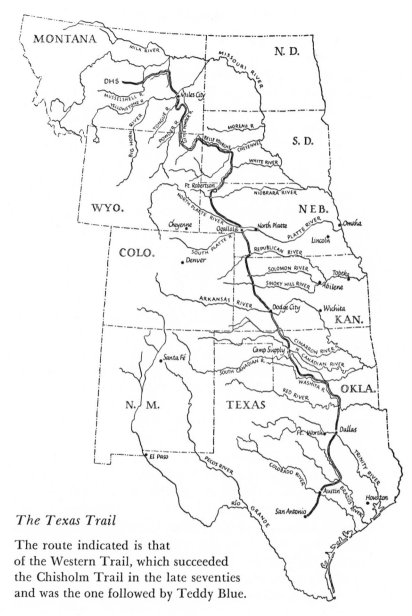

The Texas Trail

The route indicated is that
of the Western Trail, which succeeded
the Chisholm Trail in the late seventies
and was the one followed by Teddy Blue.

vii

out each time practically in identical words. He has been carving this book inside himself for years.

Teddy Blue has been interviewed repeatedly in Montana newspapers, but, except for the sketchy and incomplete versions thus given to the public, the stories told here have not been published before. Several chapters or parts of chapters which he wrote for an earlier, never-finished book are incorporated in this one. But since he has the great gift of writing exactly as he talks, there is nothing to indicate which those passages are and no reason for indicating it. Anyone who is interested in questioning the genuineness of Teddy Blue will find the documents in my possession. However, his knowledge of history will not surprise anyone who knows how common it is to find amateur historians, and good ones, among old-timers in the West. He has talked and corresponded and traded recollections endlessly, and has stored it all away.

In 1938 he was seventy-eight years old, tough as whipcord, diamond-clear as to memory, and boiling with energy. He could ride me into the ground any day when it came to work—and did, continually, during our hectic and delightful collaboration. I would knock off, exhausted, wash up for dinner, and come back to the Abbott's living room to sit down for five minutes, with my paper in another room and my pencil I didn't know where. And off he would go again. With frantic cries of "Wait a minute! Wait a minute, *please!*"—to which he paid not the slightest attention—I would dive for my paper. I came out of this with my handwriting a wreck, and a book which is all Teddy Blue. My part was to keep out of the way and not mess it up by being literary. Only the introduction and the footnotes are mine.

Because the cowboy flourished in the middle of the Victorian age, which is certainly a funny paradox, no realistic picture of him was ever drawn in his own day. Here is a self-portrait by a cowboy which is full and honest. With the idea in mind of preserving a record, I have kept close to Mr. Abbott's exact words. Nothing is so ephemeral as the language of a trade and a time; I have tried to spray a fixative on it. And of all the varieties of speech in the United States, I don't know any that for color and violence can touch the authentic Western American. In listening to the talk of these people, I have heard plenty of unconventional English but no consistency; they will use "we was" and "we were," "I done" and "I did," interchangeably in a single sentence. I have simply followed their own no-system.

As Mr. Abbott says, descriptions of scenery are not his strong point, so I will drop a hint. These reminiscences are full of rivers, and when most people read about rivers they think of trees. But you can't read this book that way. You have to remember that you are reading about a naked country with no shelter except its own folds and the low brush growing in them. Apart from occasional straggling cottonwoods, even the coulees and river bottoms are treeless, open to the sky.

In his chapter on Granville Stuart he says magnificently: "Granville Stuart was the history of Montana." Well, Teddy Blue is the history of the cattle trail and the open range.

HELENA HUNTINGTON SMITH

POSTSCRIPT: *The introduction above is reproduced for this new edition precisely as it appeared originally, when I wrote it in New York City and dated it December, 1938, except for a few changes of tense, for E. C. Abbott died in April, 1939, a few days after* We Pointed Them North *was first published.*—H.H.S.

Contents

xi

Contents

Illustrations

MAPS

We Pointed Them North

Recollections of a Cowpuncher

How I Came to Montana—The Texas Trail—
Cowboys and Cowpunchers—
No Tents, No Tarps, and Damn Few Slickers—
Sam Bass Skips Out—A Cowboy Forever

People who know me often talk as though I was from Texas. That is not correct. I was born at Cranwich Hall, Cranwich, County of Norfolk, England, December 17, 1860. But I came to Montana with a herd of Texas cattle in 1883.

That is where they get the idea that I am a Texan. All this part of Montana east of the mountains was settled by Texans who came here with the cattle, and so was Wyoming, and parts of Colorado and New Mexico, and the western half of the Dakotas, and even Nebraska before the farmers run them out. A lot of farmers and businessmen came in here after the cowpunchers, and there were a few other people who got here first. But the Texas cowboy's mode of speech and dress and actions set the style for all the range country. And his influence is not dead yet.

For a long time I have wanted to write a history of the cattle range and of the movement of the cattle as they were gradually pushed north over the Texas trail. I have read plenty of histories of the trail, written by other men who went over it, that are entirely accurate as to facts, but they are not told right. They are like these cowboy songs I have seen in books and heard over the radio, that are all fixed up and not the way we used to sing them at all. Other old-timers have told all about stampedes and swimming rivers and what a terrible time we had, but they never put in any of the fun, and fun was at least half of it. Why, even in *The Trail Drivers of Texas,* which is a wonderful book and absolutely authentic, you have all these old fellows telling stories, and you'd think they was a bunch of preachers, the way they talk. And yet some of them raised more hell than I did.

In 1922 Charlie Russell and I were going to make a book together. I was going to tell the stories and he was going to draw the pictures, and his name would have carried it. But he died. Now that I have decided to go ahead and tell the story of my life, with some history thrown in, I want to explain that as far as it goes it is accurate. There is no fiction in it. All the people mentioned are real cowmen whom I met and worked with on the cattle range that extended from southern Texas to the Bow River in Alberta, Canada. It is told entirely from my memory from 1871 to 1886, as all my papers, etc., got burnt up previous to '86. But I started in young and have lived now for sixty-eight years with the people I write of. I can remember what happened sixty years ago better than I can remember what I done yesterday.

In the seventies and eighties there were a lot of Englishmen over here playing the part of amateur cowpunchers. There were remittance men mostly, younger sons living on money that was sent them by their families, and some of them got to be real cowpunchers after awhile. But I got there by a different route. In 1871 my father came out here and settled on Section 1, Denton precinct, outside of Lincoln, Nebraska. I was the second generation and I grew up with the country, which was full of Texas cattle and Texas cowpunchers at the time. By the end of the seventies, Nebraska was getting settled up, and my father went to farming. But I stayed with the cattle and went north with them. In

1889 a good woman got her rope on me, and I have stood hitched ever since. But I am still running cattle on the 3 Deuce Ranch in Fergus County, Montana, where I have lived for the past fifty years.

When my father got over here in '71 the Texas trail had only been in existence three or four years, but it was a big business already, and a steady stream of herds was moving north. I have been told that 600,000 cattle came up to eastern Kansas and southeastern Nebraska in '71, Lincoln, Nebraska, being then the north end of the trail, because there were no ranches above that point; only Indians and buffalo. The B. & M. Railroad had got to Lincoln, and you could graze and ship the beef that was going to eastern markets, but most of the cattle were being sold in small herds to stockmen and settlers. The same applied to Abilene, Kansas. About '74–'75 the trail quit both places and moved west, on account of the country getting settled up; and after that the big cowtowns were Caldwell and Ellsworth and Dodge City, Kansas, and Ogallala, Nebraska. By 1880 Texas cattle had got as far north as Miles City, Montana, and Texas cowboys with them. The name cowpuncher came in about this time, when they got to shipping a lot of cattle on the railroad. Men would go along the train with a prod pole and punch up cattle that got down in the cars, and that was how it began. It caught on, and we were all cowpunchers on the northern range, till the close of range work.

These are familiar facts, but they tell me there are still some people who never heard them, especially in the East. There were worlds of cattle in Texas after the Civil War. They had multiplied and run wild while the men was away fighting for the Confederacy, especially down in the southern part, between the Nueces River and the Río Grande. By the time the war was over they was down to four dollars a head—when you could find a buyer. Here was all these cheap long-horned steers overrunning Texas; here was the rest of the country crying for beef—and no railroads to get them out. So they trailed them out, across hundreds of miles of wild country that was thick with Indians. In 1866 the first Texas herds crossed Red River. In 1867 the town of Abilene was founded at the end of the Kansas Pacific Railroad and that was when the trail really started. From that time on, big drives were made every year, and the cowboy was born. That Emerson Hough movie, *North of 36*, was supposed to show one of the early cattle drives to the railroad. It was pretty good, except that the moving picture people had Taisie Lockhard coming up the trail wearing pants. If the cowpunchers of them days had ever seen a woman wearing pants, they'd have stampeded to the brush.

Those first trail outfits in the seventies were sure tough. It was a new business and had to develop. Work oxen were used instead of horses to pull the wagon, and if one played out, they could rope a steer and yoke him up. They had very little grub and they usually run out of that and lived on straight beef; they had only three or four horses to the man, mostly with sore backs, because the old time saddle eat both ways, the horse's back and the cowboy's pistol pocket; they had no tents, no tarps, and damn few slickers. They never kicked, because those boys was raised under just the same conditions as there was on the trail—corn meal and bacon for grub, dirt floors in the houses, and no luxuries. In the early days in Texas, in the sixties, when they gathered their cattle, they used to pack what they needed on a horse and go out for weeks, on a cow-hunt, they called it then. That was before the name roundup was invented, and before they had anything so civilized as mess wagons. And as I say, that is the way those first trail hands were raised. Take

6

her as she comes and like it. They used to brag that they could go any place a cow could and stand anything a horse could. It was their life.

Most all of them were Southerners, and they were a wild, reckless bunch. For dress they wore wide-brimmed beaver hats, black or brown with a low crown, fancy shirts, high-heeled boots, and sometimes a vest. Their clothes and saddles were all homemade. Most of them had an army coat with cape which was slicker and blanket too. Lay on your saddle blanket and cover up with a coat was about the only bed used on the Texas trail at first. A few had a big buffalo robe to roll up in, but if they ever got good and wet, you never had time to dry them, so they were not popular. All had a pair of bullhide chaps, or leggins they called them then. They were good in the brush and wet weather, but in fine weather were left in the wagon.

As the business grew, great changes took place in their style of dress, but their boots and cigarettes have lasted nearly the same for more than sixty years. In place of the low-crowned hat of the seventies we had a high-crowned white Stetson hat, fancy shirts with pockets, and striped or checkered California pants made in Oregon City, the best pants ever made to ride in. Slickers came in too. In winter we had nice cloth overcoats with beaver collars and cuffs. The old twelve-inch-barrel Colt pistol was cut down to a six- and seven-and-a-half-inch barrel, with black rubber, ivory, or pearl handle. The old big roweled spurs with bells give place to hand-forged silver inlaid spurs with droop shanks and small rowels, and with that you had the cowpuncher of the eighties when he was in his glory.

In person the cowboys were mostly medium-sized men, as a heavy man was hard on horses, quick and wiry, and as a rule very good-natured; in fact it did not pay to be anything else. In character their like never was or will be again. They were intensely loyal to the outfit they were working for and would fight to the death for it. They would follow their wagon boss through hell and never complain. I have seen them ride into camp after two days and nights on herd, lay down on their saddle blankets in the rain, and sleep like dead men, then get up laughing and joking about some good time they had had in Ogallala or Dodge City. Living that kind of a life, they were bound to be wild and brave. In fact there was only two things the old-time cowpuncher was afraid of, a decent woman and being set afoot.

One of the first things my father did after he got over here was to go down in Texas and buy a herd of cattle. I went with him though I was only ten years old, and that was how I made my first trip up the trail. The old man never went up the trail himself—hell no, he left that to his hired hands. But I was allowed to go because I was delicate, and the idea was it would be good for my health. I was the poorest, sickliest little kid you ever saw, all eyes, no flesh on me whatever; if I hadn't have been a cowpuncher, I never would

have growed up. The doctor told my mother before we left England to "keep him in the open air." She kept me there, all right, or fate did. All my life.

We went down by train to New Orleans and then by boat to Texas. On the way back up the trail I helped wrangle the horses. I don't remember much else about the trip— only that the old man was going to tie me on my horse to cross Red River, so if the horse drownded I'd be sure to drown. I kicked like a steer, as I could swim, and the rest of them talked him out of it. We received the cattle near Red River, and afterwards I think Father took the stage back to the railroad. Anyway he left us there.

Sam Bass was my father's wagon boss. He wasn't an outlaw then—just a nice, quiet young fellow. He was with us most of the winter, but in March, '72, after the winter broke, he rode into Lincoln, where he bought a new rope, having broke his, pulling bogged cattle. In order to stretch it he was roping posts and making his horse pull it so as to get the kinks out. About that time a man walked down the board sidewalk, which was about three feet above the street. Sam roped him for a joke and pulled the rope too hard, and the old fellow stumbled and kind of cut his face in the gravel. He got up hopping mad and went for the sheriff— and Sam lit out for the ranch and got his money and pulled out for Texas. The sheriff was one hour too late.

None of us ever saw Sam Bass again. He was a nice fellow, always very kind to me, and different from most of the wild devils who came up the trail in the seventies. He did not get to drinking and raising hell. He never would have been an outlaw, only through loyalty to his boss Joe Collins, who had blowed in his whole herd in Deadwood and had to have money to face and pay his friends in Texas; so Sam helped him rob that U. P. train.

9

Three more times after that I went down to Texas and came back up the trail with a herd of cattle—in '79, in '81, and in '83. On the last of those trips I went all the way up to the Yellowstone, and when I got to Montana, I stayed. But from '71 to '78 I was tending my father's cattle around Lincoln and growing up with the men who came from Texas with them. Those years were what made a cowboy of me. Nothing could have changed me after that.

My Father—Early Days in Nebraska—
I Try to Join the Pawnees—
New Boots and a Six-shooter—A Damn Fool Kid

In a way I am the third generation of Abbotts over here. I
don't remember very much of that family history stuff. It
has always seemed a lot of damn bull to me. But my grandfather, Edward Abbott, came out here in 1848 as secretary
to Lord Ashburton, with that outfit that made the line between Canada and the United States. My grandfather was
a second son, so his older brother got everything, the way
they do in England, and my grandfather wouldn't stand for
being a gentleman pensioner, or gentleman pauper as he
called it. So he took his gun and his dog and ten pounds and
walked off, when he was a young fellow, and got a job as
gamekeeper on somebody's estate. A gentleman wasn't supposed to do any work, only join the army or the church or
something like that, but he got a contract for fixing up a
rabbit warren and made five hundred pounds. And after
that he became agent for a Sir Richard Sutton, and it was
through him, when Lord Ashburton came out here, that
he got the job as his secretary.

My grandfather went back to England with the rest of
them. But he stayed here long enough to realize what a wonderful country this would be some day. The Grand Trunk
Railway was building in eastern Canada then, and he in-

11

vested every cent he could get and made a lot of money. Twenty years later, when my father went broke in England and decided to emigrate, my grandfather made him come to Nebraska. Father had a hard time here, and to do him credit, he never wanted to come. His heart was set on South Africa, but of course he had no show to do what he wanted to do; he had to do what his father told him. That's the English of it, every time. They have to boss, boss until the day they die.

I wish I had the command of language my father had. By God, he was educated. He ought to have been a lawyer or something like that instead of a farmer. One of his brothers was a lawyer and one went into the church. But his father wouldn't let him. Can you beat it? My grandfather was a rebel himself when he was young—but he had no mercy on his son. And my father suffered from it as a young man, but when his turn came, he took it out on his children just the same. I tell you it's in the English blood to dictate, dictate. They're worse than any damn Indian that ever lived.

I never got on with my father and never pretended to. He was overbearing and tyrannical—and worse with me than with the others. I was always the one he picked on to do the chores. I remember how in the wintertime he would tell me to "coat up, coat up" and go out and feed the cattle in below-zero weather, while the rest of them were sitting around the stove. It was always "coat up, coat up"—in that overbearing way of his. And I resented it. But I got back at him too. I remember one time the butcher wanted to buy some beef, and my father was going to cut them out of the herd for him, and he asked me to give him a horse. So I caught up little Pete, my cutting horse, for him; you know a good cutting horse would turn on a dollar and was quick as a flash. Father had rode all his life on one of these flat English saddles and he thought he was a rider, but he didn't know anything about cow horses. And when he rode into the herd and started to cut out a steer, and the steer dodged back, of course Pete turned right out from under him and left him on the ground. I sure laughed. But not out loud. As it was, Father swore he'd shoot the horse, but I kept Pete out of his way for a few days and he forgot about it.

I had a hell of a row with him another time over some big Texas steers that he was breaking to sell for work oxen to people going West. We would yoke a pair of them and tie their tails together and turn them loose in a field, where they would raise hell for two or three days. One night when I was driving the herd in to pen them for the night, one yoke got to fighting and a steer got down and could not get up. I rode to the house to get help, but his neck was broke and the old man blamed me. He picked up a small pole and run at me, and if I hadn't been on a quick little Texas pony he'd have knocked me off my horse.

That was the way I was treated. And all the time I was living with Texas cowpunchers, the most independent class of people on earth, and breathing that spirit. It it hadn't been for my mother, I never would have gone back home after I was fourteen.

I told you I wasn't much on this family history stuff. I don't remember where my father had his schooling, but I think it was Cambridge, because I remember my oldest brother had a certificate showing he had passed his examinations for Cambridge when he was fourteen, and had done very well in certain subjects. He never went to Cambridge, because my father went broke and left the country. But the old man was very proud of that certificate and kept it framed in the dining room. You know, to the English, the oldest son is everything. And when my oldest brother died, my father's last hopes went with him.

I suppose that was the excuse for him, in a way. He was a misfit here. I can see now that he was not happy, though I never thought about that at the time. In England, you see, he had been a big guy. He was what they called a gentleman tenant farmer, and he ran a big place of two thousand acres over there, with thirty or forty men· working under him, and he rode around on horseback just like a planter in the South. The whole village of Cranwich was in his employ. For a man in his position it was a big comedown to have to come out here and start from nothing, and he didn't seem to have the pioneer spirit of making the best of things. He'd work hard enough—it wasn't that. He'd work with a hoe, out in the field. But he didn't seem to have any business ideas, and he kind of gave up.

He must have been forty when he came out to Nebraska, and with that education that's too old for a new country. One of his hired men would have come out here and made good and lots of them did, but he couldn't. His damned education was a detriment to him.

He was lonely, too, I guess. There was plenty of English in Nebraska, but he wouldn't associate with any of them. It was that class business Do you know what he called them? Cart-horse-bred buggers. Not that he would ever allude to his family or tell who they was or anything about them. All I know about them is what Mother told us. The girls used to brag about their noble connections, but I couldn't see and can't now what good that kind of stuff does you when you're barefoot and eating corn bread and syrup.

He always had his English newspapers, and he kept track of everything that went on back home. But as for here and

now, he wouldn't know or care if the house was six inches
deep in dirt. If it hadn't been for Mother being such a hell
of a rustler, I don't know what we'd have done—though he
was getting money from England right along.

Once he got ten thousand dollars. That was when his
father died. He got more when his mother died, and more
when his brother died, and he sunk it all in trees, and building lakes and all kinds of improvements. We figured out
that he had at least sixty thousand dollars from the time he
landed in that country, and in the end he mortgaged the
place for five thousand dollars. Oh, he paid for his mistakes.

After we got up to Nebraska with that trail herd in the
fall of '71, we ran into one of the worst winters ever known
on the range, and the loss was very heavy among the trail
cattle. The settlers had no idea how to take care of cattle;
they would put them in a pen without a shed or even a wind-
break, and I believe they lost 300,000 head of them in Nebraska and Kansas that winter, just from sheer ignorance.
Father hired a lot of hay put up at seventy-five cents a ton
out on the prairie, but he only had a small team of Texas
mules and a spring wagon to haul it, and when the snow
got deep and crusted the cattle starved and froze to death
in the corral. Next spring we had just 104 head left out of
over 300. He had shipped a lot of steers and fat dry cows to
Chicago that fall.

All during the summer of '72, when I was in my twelfth
year, I helped to hold that herd. From then on I was out on
the range, looking after my father's cattle and running wild,
when other boys my age was in school. In a way it was a
wonderful life for a boy. My mother used to say there was
gypsy blood in me, because every chance I got I would go
and visit the Indians. The Pawnee Indian reservation at
that time was north of us, on Loup River, and they would

go by our place every fall on the way out to Republican River on their annual buffalo hunt. There would be a couple of hundred Indians and twice that number of horses; everything they owned was packed on the horses, and they all had buffalo horses besides, that they only used in the chase. They would camp on the creek below us. Most of the boys could talk English and we had a big time running pony races. I was sure struck on their way of living, and so one fall I made up my mind to run away and go on the buffalo hunt.

I saw them start one afternoon, so I cached out my shotgun and two blankets and a little grub—and all the clothes I owned I had on—and I lit out on my horse in the night and caught up with them about fifteen miles away, in the morning. But when the old chief saw me he asked me: "Where go?"

I said: "With you."

He said: "No. Your father say we stole you, make plenty trouble for Indians."

And he made me go back. I was awful disappointed, but he was right, as Mother raised plenty of hell as it was, and they were out two months.

When they came back, they had over a hundred horses packed with dried buffalo meat, dried tongues, and robes. I went down to their camp and had a feast, and when they pulled out, my heart went with them. I made up my mind that as soon as I got to be a man, I would join them. But they were moved down to Indian Territory and I never saw them any more.

I did get to be a cowboy, though, and as Charlie Russell used to say, we were just white Indians anyway.

In 1873 Father bought 300 big steers from John R. Blocker, the Texas trail man, and put up lots of hay. That

Mother and Father of "Teddy Blue" Abbott

In 1876   *In 1879*

Teddy Blue

winter my older brother, Harry, would get up there and throw the hay down on my rope, and I would drag it out and scatter it for them, and then we would take them back to the pen.

That was the winter we found the dead woman in the haystack. One morning—and oh, God, it was bitter cold—Harry stuck his fork in the hay, and he struck something hard. He uncovered it, and here was this face looking up at him. He called me to come, and I got up on the haystack, and I took one look, and I lit out for home so fast I never even stopped to get on my horse. There was two hills between there and the house, and I swear I never touched but the tops of them. She had run away from the lunatic asylum—they were always doing that—with nothing on but her nightgown, and she must have crawled in the hay to get warm. The asylum was at the mouth of our creek, Haines Branch, and they'd go up through the brush toward our house.

I remember at Easter that year there came an awful blizzard that all the old-timers still tell of, that lasted forty-eight hours. Harry and me were out feeding the cattle when it struck. We were only about half a mile from the ranch, but it came so sudden we could not make it to the shed with the herd. So we let the cattle drift down to the creek where they could get a little shelter, and we huddled down in a patch of sumac brush for a time, but when it did not let up we headed for home. How we got there I never knew; I just followed my brother. When we got in, they had a rope stretched from the house to the barn, and the only way you could make it was to hold on to the rope. The snow was so thick we could hardly breathe. But I cannot remember that we was afraid at all; only that the old man would kick because we did not bring in the cattle.

Father doubled his money on those Blocker steers, and that put him on his feet until the settlers came and run him out of the cattle business. But just the same we were never well off. I never had any money when I was a kid. I never had any clothes. My mother bought me a pair of boots in '71, and because I was in the saddle all the time and never walked, hardly, they never wore out, and she wouldn't buy me another pair. Three or four years later I was still wearing them same boots, though I was a growing boy, and they had got so tight that my toes was all cramped up and skinned off, and if I had had to walk much they would have killed me. That was when my brother Harry and I were feeding the cattle in the winter, letting them out of the corral in the morning and taking them a couple of miles up the creek to where the hay was. At dinnertime we would build a fire and cook a little bacon and corn bread on a tin plate, and I would hold my feet up to the fire to warm them, because they were so cold in those tight boots it was misery. And one day I held them in the fire on purpose till they were burned, and then she *had* to buy me a new pair. I just begged her to let me put them on first, so in the end she took me to town, and we made quite an event of it and, believe me, I got them big enough.

Poor Mother. She did the best she could, but times were hard and she just didn't have the money. I give her great credit. She was raised a lady, she never had to work as a girl, she was used to having all kinds of servants—a butler, nursemaid, assistant nursemaid, and all the other help they had in those big houses. And she came out of that to a cabin on the prairie, which was nothing more than the shell of a house, without even beds to lie on in the beginning. They slept on the floor. From that time she did all the cooking and all the housework for that great big family, thirteen children before she got through, and I never heard her complain.

I lived at home every winter, as we kept the cattle there in winter. But in summer they were turned out on the range and I was out there with them, living in camp and cooking my own grub just like a man. That was how I got so friendly with Texas cowpunchers and tried to be just like them. There was always several other herds close by that I would visit and nearly all the cowboys was from Texas. And about July of every year the trail herds would start to come in, and you bet I stuck out my chest and told those men all about how *I* come up the trail.

One of the Texas fellows give me my first six-shooter, when I was about thirteen. The cylinder was burnt out, and he said: "Promise me you'll never load it." If I had, it would have blowed up in my face. He told me to just use caps with it—cap and ball. But one day I had it home, and my older brother Frank got hold of it, and he loaded it though I told him not to. It pretty near blew his hand off.

So of course my father found all about me having a gun, and he took it outside and smashed it with an ax. But that didn't change me any. As soon as I could I got another one.

Those were rough times, and we grew up rough along with them. I remember in the winter of '72–'73 old man Wade and his two sons was hanged for horse thieves. They hanged them to a whistling post on the railroad,[1] because there wasn't no trees in the damn country, and the post was low, so their feet just cleared the ground. That winter us boys talked about nothing else. My mother had a big ugly old turkey gobbler that used to chase us all the time; he knocked Frank down once. So we roped him and tied him to a wagon, and held a trial over him like we heard the vigilantes did. Then we hung him to the wagon wheel. Hell popped for awhile, but Father laughed about it all the rest of his life.

Something else that happened a little later, when I was about fourteen, will show you the kind of company I was with and the kind of ideas I was getting. I had gotten into a row at home, as I always did—it was over those steers— and I got out old Pete, my pony, and ran away, as I always did— I was going to be a cowboy this time, for sure. I got as far as Fort Kearney on the Platte, where these fellows from Texas were coming in with the trail herds. And while I was visiting at one of the camps, one of their fellows got drunk in town, and got in a shooting scrape and killed somebody. Then he fogged it back to camp, ahead of the heel flies, because he knew his friends would help him. The boss of the outfit was an old-time trail man named Matt Winters, and he came and asked me to help this fellow get away. I guess he picked me because he knew a little damn fool kid would do anything you told him. You know you can see a jack rab-

[1] Put up as a sign to the engineer to whistle for a crossing.

bit for twenty miles in that country, and when the sheriff and his posse come in sight, he told me to take a good horse and ride out on top of the ridge like I was going somewhere, and let them take after me. He said to keep ahead of them as long as I could, and stop when they started shooting, and by that time the other fellow would be on his way.

So I did just what he told me. The sheriff and his posse came along, and when they saw me on my horse, they thought sure it was this other fellow stepping out for Texas. They chased me about ten miles. And when their horses played out they started shooting, like Matt said they would, and I stopped and let them come up with me. I'll never forget the look on their faces when they found out they had run the legs off their horses just to catch me. The sheriff said: "Why, it's nothing but a God-damned tallow-faced kid!"

Charlie Russell was going to draw a picture of that for the book we was going to do together, of me standing there by my horse and all those men gathered around—but he died.

The other fellow got clean away. He waited at camp until the posse went by and then lit out in the other direction, which gave him as good as twenty miles start of them. I saw him in New Mexico about seven years later, and he give me a good horse and saddle for helping him. He was a killer, that fellow. He had killed a man before that, and he killed one after. At the time, though, he was a hero in my eyes. You know a kid looks at things differently. I thought a cowpuncher couldn't do wrong, and the sheriff was the enemy.

This sheriff was named Con Groner. He had it in for me for awhile, but in '78 I was out chasing Cheyenne Indians with him with a posse up on the North Platte River, and he got over it. Right after I pulled the trick I've been telling you about, there on the Platte, I met Gus Walker, who was a trail boss that knew me and my folks. He had shipped his beef and was taking the rest of the cattle to Lincoln, and he talked me into going back there with him. He said: "Why, your mother will be crazy over you running away."

My mad spell was about over anyway, after I had lived on two jack rabbits for three days on my way to Fort Kearney. So I wrangled his horses home, and that was the end of that runaway.

From 1874 to 1877 I was taking care of my father's cattle, and after awhile the neighbors began putting cattle with me, paying me a dollar fifty a head for six months. I herded them in the daytime and penned them at night, and for the first time in my life I could rustle a little cash. In 1875 I made twenty-nine dollars that way, and my brother Harry and I had one hell of a time. We bought a bottle of whisky, shot out the lights on the street corners, and run our horses through the streets of Lincoln whooping and yelling like Cheyenne Indians on the warpath. We'd have gone to jail sure if some of Gus Walker's trail men had not been with us. They got the blame, as everything was laid to the Texas men, but they left next day for Texas and so it all blew over. This was my first experience standing up to the bar buying drinks for the boys, and I sure felt big.

That summer, I remember, Ace Harmon, who was one of John T. Lytle's trail bosses and a god to me, said: "In a year or two Teddy will be a real cowboy." And I growed three inches and gained ten pounds that night.

3

Wild Days of the Seventies—Tough, Drunk, and Sixteen—
I Shoot a Man—An Infidel—
They Couldn't Make a Farmer of Me

From the time I was fourteen and staying out with the cattle most all the time, I got to be more and more independent. The boys took turns staying out there with me, but Lincoln was only twelve miles from camp, and when we had a little money, one of us would slip off to town on his pony, leaving the other one on herd. We'd hang around the saloons, listening to those men and getting filled up with talk about gunfights and killings. One time I remember I was in a saloon, and I heard a fellow talking about the Yankees. He said: "I was coming down the road and I met a damn blue-bellied abolitionist, and I paunched him.[1] And he laid there in the brush and belched like a beef for three days, and then he died in fits. The bastard!"

He told that before a whole crowd of men. I don't know that he ever done it. But that was the way he talked to get a fight. Those early-day Texans was full of that stuff. Most of them that came up with the trail herds, being from Texas and Southerners to start with, was on the side of the South, and oh, but they were bitter. That was how a lot of them got killed, because they were filled full of the old dope about the war and they wouldn't let an abolitionist arrest them. The marshals in those cow towns on the trail were usually

[1] Shot him through the stomach.

Northern men, and the Southerners wouldn't go back to Texas and hear people say: "He's a hell of a fellow. He let a Yankee lock him up." Down home one Texas Ranger could arrest the lot of them, but up North you'd have to kill them first.

I couldn't even guess how many was killed that way on the trail. There was several killed at every one of those shipping points in Kansas, but you get different people telling the same story over and over again and the number is bound to be exaggerated. Besides, not all that were killed were cowboys; a lot of saloon men and tinhorn gamblers bit the dust. While I saw several shooting scrapes in saloons and sporting houses, I never saw a man shot dead, though some died afterwards.

But in the seventies they were a hard bunch, and I believe it was partly on account of what they came from. Down in Texas in the early days every man had to have his six-shooter always ready, every house kept a shotgun loaded with buckshot, because they were always looking for a raid by Mexicans or Comanche Indians. What is more, I guess half the people in Texas in the seventies had moved out there on the frontier from the Southern states and from the rebel armies, and was the type that did not want any restraints.

But there is one thing I would like to get straight. I punched cows from '71 on, and I never yet saw a cowboy with two guns. I mean two six-shooters. Wild Bill carried two guns and so did some of those other city marshals, like Bat Masterson, but they were professional gunmen themselves, not cowpunchers. The others that carried two guns were Wes Hardin and Bill Longley and Clay Allison and them desperadoes. But a cowboy with two guns is all movie stuff, and so is this business of a gun on each hip. The kind

of fellows that did carry two would carry one in the scabbard and a hide-out gun down under their arm.

There was other people besides cowboys in Nebraska in
the seventies, but they was not the kind that could influence
a boy. The settlers were very religious and narrow-minded.
I remember once, me and Harry went fishing on Sunday
and caught a big catfish. One of the neighbors saw it and
had us arrested, and Father had to pay a five-dollar fine.
Most of the settlers had been Union soldiers and did not
like Texas people, and their love was returned plenty.

About this time, 1876, when I had that picture taken,
the one with the cigar in my mouth. I had a bottle of whisky
in the other hand, but it doesn't show, because I had a
fight with the other fellow in the picture and tore off his
half of it. I was drunk when the picture was made, and I
guess I wanted the world to know it. I was sixteen then and
dead tough. Oh, God, I was tough. I had a terrible reputation, and I was sure proud of it. I'll never forget the time
I walked home with a nice girl. Her people were English,
some of those cart-horse-bred English that my father looked
down on, and she had walked up to our house to visit with
the girls and stayed to supper. I took her home afterwards.
It was only about half a mile. Her family just tore her to
pieces. They saw to it she never went out with me again.

My own family wasn't taking any notice of what I was
doing. They knew I was around in saloons all the time, but
they never bothered about it, until one day an old preacher
saw me get off my horse and go into a sporting house, and
he told my father about that. The old man went up in the
air. But when he called me down for it, I stuck out my chin
and said: "Why, didn't you know?" And I told him I was
keeping a girl at one of the honky-tonks for a mistress, and
a whole lot of other big talk which wasn't true, because I

didn't have money enough to keep a mistress. My mother was behind the kitchen door listening—and I remember the old man walking out through the kitchen and saying: "Hmph! Hmph! The young fool's making fun of me. There's nothing to it."

That's the thing to do whenever you're accused of anything; make it out so much worse that nobody will believe you.

But what could he expect? He'd kept me out there with the cattle, living with all those men, and all they'd talk about was bucking horses and shooting scrapes and women. I never had a boyhood. I never had but three winters at school, and they was only parts of winters. I was a man from the time I was twelve years old—doing a man's work, living with men, having men's ideas.

And I was really dangerous. A kid is more dangerous than a man because he's so sensitive about his personal courage. He's just itching to shoot somebody in order to prove himself. I did shoot a man once. I was only sixteen, and drunk. A bunch of us left town on a dead run, shooting at the gas lamps. I was in the lead and the town marshal was right in front of me with his gun in his hand calling, "Halt! Halt! Throw 'em up!" And I throwed 'em up all right, right in his face. I always had that idea in my head—"Shoot your way out." I did not go to town for a long time afterwards, but he never knew who shot him, because it was dark enough so he could not see. He was a saloon man's marshal anyway and they wanted our trade, so did not do much about it. That was how us cowboys got away with a lot of such stunts. Besides, the bullet went through his shoulder and he was only sick a few days and then back on the job. But they say he never tried to get in front of running horses again.

But I was worse than ever afterwards. I remember about

this time there was a big banker in this Nebraska country who had been a gambler, and he had straightened out and wanted to marry a decent girl. So he began courting one of my sisters and one day he came to take her buggy riding.

I wouldn't see anything wrong with it now. But I came up and told them both to get out of that buggy or I'd shoot them out of it, and I would have. I was insulted because my sister was going around with a gambler. I wasn't going to have *my* sister talked about— and all that kind of thing.

To show you what kids can be, I had a fight with my brother Harry when I was twelve years old and he was fourteen. We tried to cut each other with knives and we made a pretty good job of it too. He had rode one of my ponies. I thought I was a cowpuncher, and it's a deadly insult to a cowpuncher to ride one of his horses without his permission. We got out our jackknives and flew at each other like a pair of little tigers. He cut me all over the hands, and I cut his chin—I was aiming at his throat. Little damned fools. And that night we slept together as though nothing had happened.

In spite of the fights we had—and that one with jackknives was the worst—Harry and I were really friends. But my oldest brother, Jimmy, was my favorite. I just worshiped him. He died when he was nineteen. I never got over it, though I was nothing but a little kid. They buried him in the cemetery in Lincoln, and the wind blowed my hat in his grave.

His death was what made an infidel of me. I asked my mother if God could have kept him from dying, and she said, yes, God was all-powerful and could have prevented it if he had wished. So I said: "I'll never go in one of your damn churches again." And I never have. That family stuffed me full of all that religious bull when I was a kid, but I never had any more use for it after I was growed, and in that I was like the rest of the cowpunchers. Ninety per cent of them was infidels. The life they led had a lot to do with that. After you come in contact with nature, you

28

get all that stuff knocked out of you—praying to God for aid, divine Providence, and so on—because it don't work. You could pray all you damn pleased, but it wouldn't get you water where there wasn't water. Talk about trusting in Providence, hell, if I'd trusted in Providence I'd have starved to death.

But the settlers would all get in their churches Sundays, and that exhorter would be hollering hell-fire and brimstone so you could hear him a mile. We'd all go to hell, the way they looked at it. If they were right there was no hope for me. You know you ride around alone at night, looking at the stars, and you get to thinking of those things.

Most of southeastern Nebraska and the whole state west of Lincoln was open range when we got there in '71, but about 1876 a flock of settlers took the country, and after that there was only a few places where you could hold cattle. Father was lucky. There was a lot of rough country adjoining him that did not get settled till '79 or '80, and he run cattle until then, but afterwards he went to farming with the rest of them. That was how I came to leave home for good when I was eighteen. I was back for visits afterwards, because I wanted to see my mother, but except for those visits my family and I went separate ways, and they stayed separate forever after. My father was all for farming by that time, and all my brothers turned out farmers except one, and he ended up the worst of the lot—a sheepman and a Republican.

But I stayed with the cattle and went north with them. You see, environment—that's a big word for me, but I got onto it—does everything for a boy. I was with Texas cowpunchers from the time I was eleven years old. And then my father expected to make a farmer of me after that! It couldn't be done.

The summer of 1878 I ran a herd of beef for some men in Lincoln, and I took them up on Cheese Creek—that was the last open range in that country. They limited me to 500 head so the cattle would do well, but they paid me twenty-five cents a head a month, and for four months I got $125 a month out of it. That was big money for a boy in those days, when the usual wages ran as low as $10, and believe me I thought I was smart. In the fall these fellows sold their cattle to feeders in the eastern part of the state and I took them down there, driving them right through the streets of Lincoln. Then I went home. After I got home my father said to me one night: "You can take old Morgan and Kit and Charlie and plow the west ridge tomorrow."

Like hell I'd plow the west ridge. And when he woke up next morning, Teddy was gone.

4

Up the Trail in '79—The Olive Outfit—
"All Horses and Men"—
Shallow Graves—Rustlers in the Nations—
My New Clothes Not Appreciated

When I pulled out in the fall of '78, I was just about broke, in spite of all the money I'd been making. Earlier that year I had went in debt for three horses, a tent, a bed, and a six-shooter and belt, and besides that I had been spending quite a lot of money on a girl. My first one. Of course she loved me. They always do as long as you've got money. I was just one more sucker on the string.

I had my bed and my war bag and stuff up in the hayloft, and I packed them on a horse that night and I drifted. Boy, I sure drifted. I went up the Platte River visiting at the different cow ranches, and I struck an outfit late in the fall that was going to take some cattle up to the Pine Ridge Indian agency in South Dakota, and I hired out for that trip. After turning over the cattle, we all went up to Deadwood to see the sights. And after that I drifted some more. I stayed awhile with a rancher I knew and then drifted south, sometimes stopping a week at a place and always welcome because I brought the news. I had almost $100 when we were paid off after delivering that beef herd, and when I got to Austin, Texas, that winter I had fifty of it left. I was being careful because it was my first time on my own, with no home to go to.

I hired out in Austin to Print Olive's outfit and came up the trail with them in the spring of '79. It was easy to get a job. The cow outfits were looking for men and every town you went into in Texas they'd tackle you to go north with a herd. You'd be leaning against the bar and one of the bosses would come up to you. "Want to go up the trail?"

"What outfit?"

"Olive outfit. Thirty dollars a month and found"—and, as the saying was, when they found you, they expected to find you in the gap.

The Olives were noted as a tough outfit—a gun outfit—which was one reason I wanted to get in with them. It would show I was tough as they were. I knew their reputation in Nebraska, and I had knowed Print Olive himself at Fort Kearney and other places, when I was hanging around the trail herds. They were violent and overbearing men, and it taken a hard man to work for them, and believe me, they had several of those all the time.

The Olive brothers, Print (I. P. Olive), Ira, Marion, and Bob was born and raised on a cow ranch about forty miles north of Austin, Texas, which was where we started from in the spring of '79. I don't know where the old man come from, but it was some place in the South. All the boys was dark, like so many Texas men of that early day, with them black eyes just like a rattlesnake's and a temper to match. It was told that Print had killed nine niggers. Now I couldn't swear as to that number being right, but there is no doubt about it, they were a tough crowd.

About '77 or '78 they had put in a lot of cattle on the South Loup River in western Nebraska, and they was always on the trail with a half a dozen herds. The year I went with them I was told they drove 7,000 horses north, and I don't know how many head of cattle. Print himself was in Nebraska that summer waiting to stand trial for the murder of some settlers, so his brother Ira was the head trail boss. While I liked Print and Marion all right, I never did like Ira, and that was the reason for an incident, I suppose you would call it, that happened on the trail. To show you the kind of man Ira was, when the Olives first moved north, they built a big corral on the Republican River, called the Olive pens, because like so many Texas men at that time they would pen their herd at night. Ira gave orders to have one man ride his horse and set right in the gate to make the cattle come out slow, so they would not jam and knock off their horns. One morning he found several horns in the gate, and he cussed a Mexican named Leon, who pulled his knife out of his boot to throw it. Ira shot him dead. Afterwards he paid Leon's widow a lot of money and nothing was done. All this happened before I joined the outfit, but coming up in '79 he started to pull the same thing on a nigger named Kelly. One morning Ira got on the prod and started to cuss Kelly, and the first thing he hit him in the mouth with his gun, knocking out two teeth. He wanted Kelly to reach for his gun so he could kill him. I told him if he hit that boy again I would shoot his damn eyes out.

I was a fool all right, but I wasn't scared of nothing in those days. I was just looking for that kind of a rep. Besides, he knew he was wrong, and that helped me out. He put his gun in the scabbard, got on his horse and left the herd, and I never saw him again till '82. He just rode from one herd to another anyhow.

That was the only trouble I ever had in the outfit. The Olives was mostly hard on Mexicans and niggers, because being from Texas they was born and raised with that intense hatred of a Mexican, and being Southerners, free niggers was poison to them. But they hired them because they worked cheaper than white men. This Kelly that I was telling about was quite a character. They called him Olive's bad nigger, because he was a gunman and fighter himself. The Olives used to send him ahead to talk turkey to the settlers; where one of these fellows had taken up a homestead on good water, not to work it you understand, but just so he could charge the trail herds a big fee. They were doing that all along the trail, especially in Kansas; it was just a graft, but a lot of the bosses would pay what they asked rather than have trouble. The Olives never would. They would send Kelly, and that big black boy with his gun would sure tell them punkin rollers where to head in at. He'd roll up his eyes like a duck in a thunderstorm and grit his teeth—Lord, he could play a tune with his teeth. Most of the settlers were poor Northern folks that had never seen many niggers and was scared of them anyway, and when they saw Kelly they would come down quick enough from twenty dollars to five dollars as the price for watering the herd.

As for Print, it was the year before I come up the trail that he had his run-in with the settlers in Nebraska, and they got him for it, too, though he was not all to blame. It started because some of those fellows was butchering his steers and selling them for elk meat. Print got his brother appointed stock inspector, and he found out that two men named Ketchum and Mitchell was doing the butchering. When they went to arrest the two men, Bob Olive was killed. Rather than face Print's vengeance the two settlers give themselves up to be tried, and to make a long story short, Print followed them up when they was on their way to trial, took them away from the sheriff, and hanged them to a lone elm tree near Plum Creek. It was told afterwards that he poured coal oil on them and burned them alive. That was a damned

34

lie. They were burnt all right, but a man who was there told me that when they were hanging Print shot them, and the powder was what set their clothes on fire. Afterwards their clothes was analyzed, and the state's attorney claimed that there was coal oil showing. But where would you find a farmer without some coal oil on his clothes? And why would Print have stopped for coal oil, in a hurry like he was? Print was a bad actor, and I ain't out to make excuses for him, but he had my sympathy there.

The burned bodies of those two settlers was put on exhibition, and the excitement was something fierce. All the cowboys was on the side of Print, and during the trial they came from all over to take him out of jail. But Mrs. Olive begged them not to because it would make an outlaw of him. I went to see him in the penitentiary afterwards. He was just like a caged lion, fit to tear himself to pieces. When he had been in there a year, maybe two, the judge let him out on a writ of error, and he went free after that. But it broke him. He was killed in Trail City, Colorado, in '86, over a ten-dollar livery bill a cowboy owed him.

That trip up the trail in '79 was my second, but in a way it was the first that counted, because I was only a button the other time. I wasn't nineteen years old when I come up the trail with the Olive herd, but don't let that fool you. I was a man in my own estimation and a man in fact. I was no kid with the outfit but a top cowhand, doing a top hand's work, and there is nothing so wonderful about that. All I'd ever thought about was being a good cowhand. I'd been listening to these Texas men and watching them and studying the disposition of cattle ever since I was eleven years old.

Even in years I was no younger than a lot of them. The average age of cowboys then, I suppose, was twenty-three or four. Except for some of the bosses there was very few thirty-year-old men on the trail. I heard a story once about a school teacher who asked one of these old Texas cow dogs to tell her all about how he punched cows on the trail. She said: "Oh, Mister So-and-So, didn't the boys used to have a lot of fun riding their ponies?"

He said: "Madam, there wasn't any boys or ponies. They was all horses and men."

Well, they had to be, to stand the life they led. Look at the chances they took and the kind of riding they done, all the time, over rough country. Even in the daytime those deep coulees could open up all at once in front of you, before you had a chance to see where you were going, and at night it was something awful if you'd stop to think about it, which none of them ever did. If a storm come and the cattle started running—you'd hear that low rumbling noise along the ground and the men on herd wouldn't need to come in and tell you, you'd know—then you'd jump for your horse and get out there in the lead, trying to head them and get them into a mill before they scattered to hell and gone. It was riding at a dead run in the dark, with cut banks and prairie dog holes all around you, not knowing if the next jump would land you in a shallow grave.

I helped to bury three of them in very shallow graves. The first one was after a run on the Blue River in '76. I was working for my father then, herding cattle outside Lincoln, and this outfit that had the run was part of a Texas trail herd belonging to John Lytle. He had sold five hundred cows to an Englishman named Jones—Lord Jones, they called him—on the Blue River. Three of Lytle's men were delivering the cows, and they took me along to help them because I knew the country, though I was only fifteen years old. We were camped close to Blue River one night, near a big prairie dog town that was the furthest east of any prairie dog town I ever saw—it's from there on to the Rockies that you strike them.

And that night it come up an awful storm. It took all four of us to hold the cattle and we didn't hold them, and when morning come there was one man missing. We went back to look for him, and we found him among the prairie dog holes, beside his horse. The horse's ribs was scraped bare of hide, and all the rest of horse and man was mashed into the ground as flat as a pancake. The only thing you could recognize was the handle of his six-shooter. We tried to think the lightning hit him, and that was what we wrote his folks down in Henrietta, Texas. But we couldn't really believe it ourselves. I'm afraid it wasn't the lightning. I'm afraid his horse stepped into one of them holes and they both went down before the stampede.

We got a shovel—I remember it had a broken handle—and we buried him near by, on a hillside covered with round, smooth rocks that we called niggerheads. We dug a little ground away underneath him and slipped his saddle blanket under him and piled niggerheads on top. That was the best we could do. The ground was hard and we didn't have no proper tools.

But the awful part of it was that we had milled them cattle over him all night, not knowing he was there. That was what we couldn't get out of our minds. And after that, orders were given to sing when you were running with a stampede, so the others would know where you were as long as they heard you singing, and if they didn't hear you they would figure that something had happened. After awhile this grew to be a custom on the range, but you know this was still a new business in the seventies and they was learning all the time.

Coming up the trail in '81 we had a man killed in a big

mix-up on the Washita, in the Nations, when six or seven herds was waiting for the river to go down, and a storm come and they all run together one night. And when I was coming up in '83, a man was killed in another outfit, going over a cut bank in broad daylight. His name was Davis, and he had a nickname I couldn't even tell you. He was with a roundup outfit on the French Fork of Republican River, right where the trail crosses it. We pulled in to water at noon, and we could see the roundup working further up the creek. It seems that two of them were trying to rope a dim-branded steer, and he went over a thirty-foot cut bank, and they both went over after him. Davis was a dally welter,[1] and he had lost his rope; he was reaching down to pick it up, at a gallop, and he didn't see what was coming. The second man saw it in time. He pulled his horse's head way up, and he lit more or less right side on top. It shook him up something terrible and he spent a long time in the hospital, but he lived through it. Davis was killed deader than hell.

The roundup boys saw all this happen. When they got down there, a rider taken him up in front of his saddle and carried him to camp in his arms. Our outfit laid off that afternoon to rest the herd and help bury him, and I remember after we got the grave dug one of the fellows said: "Somebody ought to say something. Don't nobody know the Lord's Prayer?" I said: "I do." So they asked me to say it over him, but I only got as far as "Thy will be done," and got to thinking about my brother and had to quit. You know why. I was kind of rattled anyhow.

Coming up in '79, we ran into rustlers in the Nations. These fellows were Mexicans and some good-for-nothing

---

[1] A roper who wraps the end of his rope around the saddle horn, Oregon style, instead of tying it fast the way the Texans do. From the Spanish, *de la vuelta*.

white men and half-breeds, who picked on the trail herds after they crossed Red River. They would follow you up for days with a pack horse, waiting their chance and keeping out of sight among the hills. A dark night was what they were looking for, especially if it was raining hard, because the rain would wash out the tracks—they'd figured all that out. They would watch you as you rode around the herd on night guard—always two men, and you rode to meet—and then when the two of you come together they would slip up to the other side of the herd and pop[2] a blanket. And the whole herd would get up like one animal and light out. These rustlers had very good horses, and they would cut in ahead of you as you tried to get up in front of the herd, and would cut off anywhere from fifty to two hundred head of big, strong lead steers.

Our outfit saw them just after they had popped the blanket. The fellows on night herd started shooting, and the rest of us woke up and grabbed for our horses. It's funny how long ago it seems. All I remember is a wild goose chase. The rustlers just left our little night horses, and of course they got away with the cattle. But next morning another fellow and I cut for sign and we found their trail. We fol-

2 Wave.

lowed it until we saw a man's hat sticking up over the top of a hill. And on the other side of the hill we found our steers.

We hit the Western trail that trip, crossing Red River at Doan's store, and we came on up to Loup River in Nebraska and turned the cattle over there. After that I went home to see my mother. I had been away a solid year. No, I hadn't wrote to her. Didn't have nothing to tell her—didn't want any of them to know where I was. I was her pet and all that, but she was always bullyragging me about drinking and spending my money in town, and so on—afraid I was going to turn out bad. I thought I knew more than she did. And I didn't know straight up.

But before I went home, I stopped in North Platte, where they paid us off, and bought some new clothes and got that second picture taken. There is nothing long ago about that. I remember it like it was yesterday. I had a new white Stetson hat that I paid ten dollars for and new pants that cost twelve dollars, and a good shirt and fancy boots. They had colored tops, red and blue, with a half-moon and star on them. Lord, I was proud of these clothes! They were the kind of clothes top hands wore, and I thought I was dressed right for the first time in my life. I believe one reason I went home was just so I could show them off.

But when I got there and my sister saw me, she said: "Take your pants out of your boots and put your coat on. You look like an outlaw."

I told her to go to hell. And I never did like her after that. Those were the first store clothes I had ever bought myself. Before that my mother made my clothes or they were bought for me, just like you'd do for a kid.

My sister was a fool anyhow.

Sagebrush and Mexicans—Wet Horses—
I Get Little Billy—
The Rattlesnake Wins—With John Chisum on the Pecos—
A Woman Outlaw

In the spring of 1880 I hired out to the C Y, a Wyoming outfit, to go into Oregon and bring back some cattle for them over the mountains. Lots of cattle were being trailed in from Oregon to stock the range country, almost as many as from Texas; but as things turned out, I never saw Oregon that year, nor ever would have if it hadn't been for Mama and me going to visit some relatives in Seattle in 1928.

The owner of the C Y was Judge Carey, later Senator Carey of Wyoming. Two of his bosses wintered in Lincoln in '79–'80, because one of them was stuck on a girl down there, and they hired me and four or five other fellows to go up and bring these cattle over the mountains, and we were supposed to rendezvous in Cheyenne. But we had only been waiting around there a few days when we run onto a fellow who had been to Oregon, and he got strung out on the awful weather—said it had rained on him for three solid weeks coming over the same trail the year before. That didn't sound any too good, so another fellow and I made up our minds to quit the layout and go to New Mexico instead. We taken the train and went south, and I have cussed myself ever since.

We stayed in Denver a few days and then went down

41

on a construction train to Conejos, close to the New Mexico line. The D. & R. G. was building then, and it only runs trains as far as Conejos—or San Antonio rather, which is what the station was called. The summer of '80 was celebrated as a hot, dry summer even in that country, and to show you what that country was like they told a story about a tough guy who got killed there, and as soon as he got to hell, he wired back for his overcoat. From what I went through, I believe it. The Río Grande was boiling mud, the sand drifted like snow does in Montana, and it was hotter than hell. We stayed around awhile in Conejos, which was a little 'dobe town and no pleasure resort. The next town up the San Luis Valley was Alamosa, over thirty miles of those damn sandy sagebrush flats where the sage grows as tall as a man's head on horseback, and you can't even look around you and see where you are riding. All I ever seen in that country, except sagebrush, was Mexicans and goats, and I never did have a high opinion of Mexicans. They'll *carrajo* around until they find out the other fellow can shoot with a gun, and then they just aren't there.

After we had been down there about a week, my partner quit. He was from North Adams, Massachusetts, so he was a long way from home. His father was a big civil engineer; it was another case of wanting to be a cowboy; he had stuck it out for four years in Nebraska, but when it come to the Southwest he couldn't take it as well as I could—the water warm and bad, and dust gritting in everything you ate. He had more money than guts, but I don't know as I blamed him when he bought a ticket back to Nebraska.

I won enough at a monte game in Conejos to buy a horse, and I had my saddle. Right after that I met a man who was going down into New Mexico to receive a big herd of horses, and he hired me to go along. His name was Bill

Charlton, and I had knowed him before in Nebraska. He was a tall, dark man, and a gambler by nature like so many of these big cattlemen; from California originally, but at this time running a big ranch at Saltillo, twelve or fifteen miles from Lincoln. We rode down the Río Grande three hundred miles, and got to the place where we were to receive the horse herd. There was seven hundred head of them, and they was sure enough wet horses—meaning that they was stolen in old Mexico and swum across the Río Grande. Four Mexicans was in charge of the herd, and Bill counted out the money to them on a blanket in four yellow piles of gold. There was all kinds of brands on those horses. I believe some of them had been raised in Texas and stolen the other way first. Bill told me he was paying three dollars a head for them and taking them into Nebraska to sell them to the settlers. And while I never finished out the trip, I saw Bill in Miles City, Montana, three years later, and he told me he disposed of them horses for twenty-five and thirty dollars apiece.

They were very tired when we met them, as they had been pushed hard. So as we were on fair feed and water, we let them rest about ten days, then started north up the river with them. There were five of us with the outfit, four white men and a Mexican. The Mexican broke horses and we rode second, after he kind of took the buck out of them, and we were riding them all the time as we went along. One day I saw the Mexican breaking a little bay horse and learning him to start quick in a race. He would get down and make a mark with his foot in the dust, then get on and say, "Go." They called that learning to score. Also he was learning him to bump the other horse with his shoulder at every jump. The little bay was quick as a flash to start and could run like a deer.

43

One morning Bill Charlton was riding a half-broke horse, and he couldn't ride very good. The horse cut up some, and Bill got mad and spurred him. At that time they all had these Mexican spurs with long rowels and bells on them, and a long hook—the cinch hook it was called—on top of the rowel; this was to hook into them leather bands, when a horse was bucking, and keep you from being throwed. Now Bill accidentally ran this hook into the cinch ring, and it caught there, and the horse bucked him off. He would have been kicked to death in a minute. I was riding a green horse myself, but I got alongside Bill's horse and grabbed the cheek strap and throwed myself out of the saddle. But my own spur caught on the cantle, and there I was stretched out for about a second between them two horses. Then I got loose and dropped to the ground, and got the cinches unbuckled and the saddle off and Bill out if it.

He was pretty well shaken up, and he thanked me. He said: "What have I got you want?"

I said: "Give me that little bay horse."

He said: "Hell, take a good horse." But I wanted the little bay. So he gave him to me, and that was how I got little Billy—named after Bill Charlton— that was my top horse for twenty-six years.

The next day I caught him up to ride, and he showed me a thing or two. He started to buck, and first my six-shooter went, then my Winchester went, then I went, and he finished up by bucking the saddle over his head. After that I would not have taken a million dollars for him. He was about ten years old when I got him, and was thirty-six years old when he died on this ranch of old age. He was a wonderful rope and cut horse, but I thought so much of

44

him I never used him much, only to ride him to town. That was the reason he lasted so long.

My arm was never really the same after that stretching. In a couple of years rheumatism set in where the ligaments was torn, and I always had to have somebody saddle my horse for me on bad mornings. That was the price I paid for little Billy.

After we crossed into Colorado a lot of different things happened and I left Bill Charlton's horse outfit, and I got very sick with mountain fever. When I got better of that, I left my horse in a small town called La Veta and taken the train to Denver, where I had some friends. As I was still weak from the fever, I couldn't do much, but just stayed with a man named Frank Ward who run a saloon. Both him and his wife were very kind to me, and I tended bar when he wanted to go out.

One day a man walked in the saloon carrying a big glass jar with a live rattlesnake in it. He wanted to sell it. Frank says: "Hell, no, they see snakes soon enough."

But the man kept arguing with him. He says: "It's big money for you if you'll buy it. Now I'll bet the drinks for the house there ain't a man here that can hold his finger on that glass and keep it there when the snake strikes."

To show you what a bonehead I was, I took him up. It was thick glass and I knew damn well the snake couldn't bite me, so I put my finger on it. The snake struck, and away come my finger. I got mad and made up my mind I would hold my finger on that glass or bust. It cost me seventeen dollars before I quit, but since then I've never bucked the other fellow's game and it has saved me a lot of money.

Frank bought the snake and he sure made money on it. It was lots of fun to get some sucker that thought he was long on nerve to go against it; no one ever could. But one night a bunch of cowboys came in and I knew some of them. They all tried the snake and failed, and one of them got mad and busted the glass with his six-shooter, and the snake got out and they had to kill it.

That was a big night in more ways than one. We all got well lit up and went to a hot show on Blake Street. The play I think was called "Poor Nell"; anyway, a burglar beats his wife to death on the stage. After he had knocked her down he taken hold of her hair and beat her head on the floor, and every time he struck her head he would stamp his foot. It sounded like her head hitting the floor, but it wasn't her head at all. I was sober enough to know that. But some of them weren't. Bill Roden, one of the cowboys, had went to sleep but the noise woke him up, and the first thing he saw was the man beating the woman's head on the floor. We sat right in front, and he gave one jump onto the stage and busted the fellow on the head with his six-gun before he remembered where he was. The woman got up and began to cuss him, all hell broke loose, somebody pulled Bill off the stage, they called for the police, the boys shot out the lights, and everybody broke their necks getting away from there. They all run to Bailey's corral where the horses were and got away before the police knew who to arrest. I made a sneak down an alley to Frank's place, got what few dollars I had, and left town on foot.

That night I got to a station eight miles away and taken the train to La Veta, where I got little Billy, and that was the last of Colorado for me. From there I drifted on down to New Mexico, where I worked for John Chisum on the Pecos awhile.

I guess I missed a chance while there to see some history in the making, but that piece of history didn't appeal to me, and I got out *muy pronto*. The Lincoln County troubles was still going on, and you had to be either for Billy the Kid or against him. It wasn't my fight and I wasn't for or against, though cowpunchers as a class never had any use for Billy the Kid—it was the Mexicans that made a hero of him. He had fell out with Chisum the year before, after being on his side in the war, over $500 that the Kid claimed Chisum owed him. The talk there at the time was that the Kid told Chisum: "I will kill one of your men for every fifty dollars you owe me," and that he had already killed three and sent Chisum the receipt.

I worked on the fall roundup and helped move some cattle, and then I quit. I remember I spent Christmas day on the bank of the Pecos, with my horse Billy and a little fire for company. That was one desolate country and I never wanted to go back. But they say that now they raise four crops of alfalfa there a year.

I was on my way to El Paso when I built that Christmas

fire. I got there in January, and oh, boy, that was a wide-open town. The railroad was coming and always ahead of it there comes these tent saloons and honky-tonks, a whole army of them. Jim Gillett was the city marshal and Dallas Stoudenmire if I remember rightly was the U. S. marshal, and they were both good fellows and good friends of mine. But while I was there I seen a little bit more shooting than I cared about, and it more or less turned me against the whole idea.

You see I had a friend down there and he got in a mix-up. Four or five Mexican outlaws came across the river one night to have a drink and raise hell, and Gillett wanted to arrest them, and he called on everybody to help. Of course my friend throwed in with him. It was none of his fight in a way, but that was our religion in those days—"Stay with your friends." When the smoke cleared away, the four Mexicans was lying dead on the floor.

And that wasn't the worst of it. One of the Mexicans that was shot turned out to be a woman dressed up in man's clothes. This fellow I knew went to turn her over, and she was just dying and she looked up at him and he never could forget that look, or the way he felt when he saw it was a woman. He knew he hadn't been the one that killed her because she was shot through the body and he always aimed at the head—he'd been educated that way. An old Texas cowpuncher told him—and a murderous old cus he was— "You always want to shoot 'em in the right eye because that disturbs their aim."

But even though he felt sure he hadn't killed the woman, he felt sick and disgusted with the whole business. Also the dead Mexicans had plenty of relatives still living, and those Mexicans have long memories and a revengeful disposition, and some of them may be alive yet. This fellow was in a spot because he didn't even have the excuse of being an officer, so he figured that El Paso was not a healthy place for him any more.

I left El Paso myself about that time—didn't like it there anyway. And I got with another trail herd going north. John B. Blocker bought the herd in Ogallala, and, after we turned them over, I went home once more.

Riding the Range in '82—
Buffalo Bill Upsets a Roundup—
Johnny Stringfellow Falls off the Water Wagon—
Dry Drives—I Drink Alkali and Eat Coyote

The fall of '81 I stayed around home, because I would be twenty-one in December and I had $3,000 coming to me. An old uncle of ours who died in England had left this much money to each of us when we were twenty-one. The year before, down in the Southwest, I had seen a place I wanted; it belonged to a Mexican in Colorado. It was a ranch in a box canyon, and by running a fence across the mouth of it and patching up the rim rocks a little bit, you could run a lot of cattle in there. When I got home from New Mexico I told my father about this place and asked him to give me my money early.

He said: "You'll get your money when you're twenty-one and not before, and by the time you are twenty-five it will all be gone, and you'll know then that you're a damn fool."

And three years later, up here in Montana, the money was all gone, and I told another fellow about it and I said: "I'm twenty-four and I know already that I'm a damn fool."

After I got the money I bought a small bunch of cattle with it the first thing; I had had enough of the wild life and intended to settle down. But it did not work out that way. That winter I got lung fever and nearly died coughing. I coughed up a small bullet that was shot into me in '80, and after that I soon got well. But the sickness got me to drinking again, and I went in and cut a big swathe in town, most of the time with one girl. I do not mean that she was a decent girl; we knew very few of those. In April I saw I would have to get out of there, so I rode off and went west to the Loup River and went to work for the Olive outfit again. And they sent me riding with Bill Cody's wagon to gather stray cattle clear down to the North Platte.

That summer Buffalo Bill himself came out to visit the beef roundup in a spring wagon loaded with whisky and beer, and he sure raised hell with that roundup. He had everybody running horse races and shooting at marks instead of gathering beef, and he offered $100 to the first man who would rope a jack rabbit; and Jesse Reeves of the Heart outfit on Snake River did rope a jack rabbit. Pretty soon he went to North Platte for some more whisky, and we did not do any work for a week. They ship the beef early in Nebraska, in August, and here was Bill Paxton and other owners of big outfits chewing their mustaches in Ogallala, with cars all ready and waiting for the herds to come in. At last they come out to see what was wrong. They fired Buffalo Bill off the roundup in a hurry, and we sure got a gait on us to gather and ship them beef.

Bill Cody at that time was half-owner of the C N outfit, Cody and North, with headquarters at North Platte City. He lived there for years. He was a good fellow, and while he was no such great shakes as a scout as he made the eastern people believe, still we all liked him, and we had to hand it to him because he was the only one that had brains enough to make that Wild West stuff pay money. I remember one time he came into a saloon in North Platte, and he took off his hat, and that long hair of his that he had rolled up under his hat fell down on his shoulders. It always bothered him, so he rolled it up and stuck it back under his hat again, and Brady, the saloon man, says: "Say, Bill, why the hell don't you cut the damn stuff off?"

And Cody says: "If I did, I'd starve to death."

Ogallala was a live town that fall. There was a whole lot of people coming and going, and trail herds getting up there from Texas, and lots of big doings that did not amount to much in a serious way, but made good stories to tell up and down the range. That fall was the time Jake Des Rosses put the woman's drawers on at a dance, and it was also the time Johnny Stringfellow fell off the water wagon.

This Stringfellow was one of the very best cowhands that ever was born, but he had one weakness which was not unusual with cowmen of that day or any other; he could not stay away from the bottle. He was foreman for Bill Paxton, who owned the Keystone outfit on the North Platte, near Ogallala, and Bill felt so serious about Johnny's drinking that he offered him one hundred head of beef—"and you can cut 'em"[1]—if he would stay sober for a year.

I don't know how long the offer had stood, but it wasn't more than a couple of months, when Johnny got into Ogallala with the rest of the gang, shipping beef. And they got him to dealing a monte game one night, and he won so much at first that he got excited and started drinking. And the more he drunk and won the more excited he got, and when they asked him "what limit," he pointed to the ceiling. Pretty soon the word got round, and Bill Paxton came to the door to remind Johnny of his offer. And Johnny told him where to go with his beef, because, he says: "I'll be able to buy you out before morning."

---

[1] Meaning that he could pick out the best in the herd. It was a handsome offer. At current cattle prices it was worth $3,500 to $4,000.

Riding the Range in '82

They said Bill was so sore he got on the train that night and went to Omaha. But he might just as well, because nobody could do nothing with Johnny. There was a good percentage for the dealer in that game, and if he had played a limit and stayed sober he could have kept ahead. But instead he kept doubling the bets, and they swamped him. In the cold gray daylight next morning another wagon boss by the name of Johnny Burgess was coming along the street— and Burgess hadn't shipped yet, and he never touched a drop until he'd shipped his herd. And here was Johnny Stringfellow with his arm around a telegraph pole, tapping on it with the handle of his six-shooter. Burgess said: "What on earth are you doing?"

And String said: "I'm telegraphing to Bill Paxton for more money."

That story caused many a laugh among cowmen. But it shows you what kind of a relation there could be, in the days of the big cow outfits, between a boss like Bill Paxton and a foreman like Johnny Stringfellow. The next fall, '83, Bill sold his outfit to the Ogallala Land and Cattle Company, and Johnny was out of a job, but when they parted, Bill gave him $500. He thought the world and all of that little man. And perhaps, after what I've told you, you wonder why.

But a foreman like Johnny was worth an awful lot of money to an outfit, and that offer of one hundred beef was no foolishness, because if he'd stayed sober, he'd have more than made it up in the way he handled the herd. You've no idea how easy it is to knock a dollar off a beef; your profit all depends on moving them along quiet and easy, and with those wild cattle it took kid gloves; in the old days if you'd get a herd of beef to the railroad and get them penned without a run, the bosses would buy every man in the outfit a new suit of clothes. When it come to keeping the tallow

53

on 'em, Johnny Stringfellow was ace high. I've never seen a man that handled cattle as smooth as he did, just as smooth as silk, and he handled men the same way. There wasn't a man in his outfit that wouldn't go to hell for him. He was a little bit of a fellow with one eye out. And you couldn't know him without loving him.

They tell a story about Johnny, when he first came up from Texas with the Cody and North outfit, that shows a lot about cowpuncher nature. He was surely a typical cowhand. You know cowhands hated to do any kind of work that could not be done on horseback; they were all like an old Mexican I knew up here in Montana by the name of Rafael. This Rafael—the only Mexican I ever knew that I liked—he came up here to the northern range with his trail boss, who he thought so much of he wouldn't leave him. When the outfit located up here, they put Rafael to work digging an irrigation ditch, and the second day somebody rode out to where he was sweating with a shovel and asked him how he was coming, and he wiped his face and said: "No lika dis class of bees-ness."

Neither did Johnny. When the C N outfit got up to Nebraska and turned the herd loose on the Dismal Fork of Loup River, the next thing they had to do was build houses and barns and so forth, so they put Johnny to work cutting down trees. This was a job he had never tackled before, only to get a little wood for a campfire. He got blisters on his hands and he come near cutting his foot off, and pretty soon he come around to the boss, Frank North, and said "Is this all you've got for me to do?"

North said: "Why, yes, I'm afraid so. These buildings have got to be built."

Johnny said: "All right. Then I might as well go to Ogallaly and punch out the other eye, and get me a monkey and an organ and go at this right." And he quit. Bill Cody told me about it himself. Now I couldn't swear that the rest of this story is true, but they used to tell that after Johnny left, a Frenchman came in there trapping beaver and he asked if he could set traps and they said sure, go ahead, but there wasn't any beaver on the Dismal Fork. And he pointed to Johnny's trees and said: "There must be beaver"—because they looked like they had been chewed down.

Oh, he had his faults, Johnny did, and being a poor hand with an ax was not the worse of them. He never could hang onto a dollar. After Bill Paxton sold out the Keystone outfit, Johnny came up here to Miles City, where he blowed the five hundred Paxton gave him, and he spent the winter with me at the F U F—I was in Montana by that time—flat broke. Next spring the F U F hired him as trail boss to go down and bring up another herd, and he came up to Miles City again in the fall of '84, and they made him boss of the outfit up here. But in time whisky and gambling got him so it was a sad thing to see. They even say that his last year with the F U F they found him laying drunk under the wagon *before* he'd shipped. It wouldn't have mattered what he done after.

Yet even after he got to going downhill so bad he couldn't hold an outfit, there was people who stood by him for what he had been and what, in a way, he still was. And one of those people was Colonel Seth Mabry, who had sent hundreds of thousands of cattle up the trail. He was a two-fisted, hard-boiled old son of a gun—in its day his outfit was known as a gun outfit, like the Olives'—but he was dead stuck on Stringfellow. And after Johnny couldn't get a job any more, Colonel Mabry staked him to a little bunch of cattle on Powder River, and as far as I know he stayed there until he died.

There are so many stories to tell about just the range itself and the way we used to handle the cattle that I could fill a whole book with nothing but that, without putting in any of my own part of it. You can read a lot in books about dry country and alkali and so forth, but those things don't mean nothing to people traveling like they do today, in a car going sixty miles an hour. To know what it is to be dry; to know what them sandy gulches mean, instead of the nice creek bottoms with a little muddy water in them that you'd find in halfway decent country, you would have to trail a herd of cattle across a dry stretch, with their tongues hanging out and slaver running out of their mouths. Later even the spit dries up, the same as with human beings. Fifteen miles a day if you push hell out of them, across a dry stretch of maybe forty miles that you'd jump over in a car without even knowing it was there. One of the worst dry drives I ever remember was up here in Montana in the fall of '86, when we were moving a lot of cattle across the Missouri River. There wasn't a drop of water between Box Elder Creek and the Missouri, forty miles of badlands and alkali. It was a hot, dry fall and no wind; two or three herds had went ahead of us and the alkali dust hung solid in the air. My partner's lips were cracked open and bleeding. I told him to stop licking them. Remember that if you're ever where it's dry; don't lick your lips.

In making a dry drive, after you left the last water you would keep them walking until way into the night before you let them bed down, because they would not get so thirsty in the cool of the night. Next morning as soon as it was daylight you would have them on the trail, and you'd keep it up all that day and half the night again, and part of the next day.

If they smell water when they are dry, they are going to it and Christ can't hold them. That was how Harry Landers, one of the best trail bosses in the business, lost his herd in '82. They were coming up to Green River, in Wyoming, on their way to Powder River; coming from Oregon, and it was right at the end of a forty-mile dry drive. He should have held up the lead and kept his cattle together, but instead he left them, and took the wagon and horses, and went ahead to the river. When the river was not more than a mile or two in front of them, the wind came down from a big bend away up stream, all of twenty-five or thirty miles away. And they threw up their heads and sniffed, the boys told me, and they all turned like one cow and started toward it on a trot. It took a day to get them back on the trail again.

I have heard cowmen argue about how far cattle could smell water when they were dry. Ben Reeves, trail boss for the L S, told me that one time his cattle smelt the Missouri River forty miles away. North of Miles City, it was, and I know that's dry country. There was a little bit of a spring to the east of where they was, and no other water from there to the Missouri, forty miles north. But a breeze came down from the north, and those cattle throwed up their heads and started walking. He got them turned to the spring all right, but they weren't really dry. They don't get bad until the second day.

I have been hungry and thirsty myself plenty of times, but all the rest was a picnic compared to one time in the summer of '82, in the Nebraska sand hills. After I went to work for the Olive outfit again, like I told you, this other fellow and I were sent out with a string of eight horses apiece to rep with Bill Cody's outfit on the roundup. They told us they would be camped on a certain lake in the sand hills, and we was to join them there. So we rode all one day, about

57

forty miles,[2] but when we got to the place they were supposed to be, they weren't there and the lake was dry.

We hadn't brought no grub. We expected to find the outfit, and cowboys don't carry box lunches. So we made camp that night without food or water. Next morning we started out again, expecting to find them at another lake we knew about, that was another day's ride away. It was just like the day before, only that much worse. No water and nothing to eat. We couldn't even kill a jack rabbit. There was no game in there except antelope—and we couldn't get close enough to those to get a shot at them. The first day you want a drink awful bad. The second day you can't think of nothing else—can't talk—can't spit. You've just got to keep going, and you rope a fresh horse every couple of hours, and you go along at a high trot, pounding that saddle.

About five or six o'clock at night we found this other little lake we were looking for, and there was some water in it. About six inches deep, swimming with polliwogs, and coffee-colored with alkali. We strained out the polliwogs through a handkerchief and tried to drink it. The alkali was so strong we couldn't keep it on our stomachs. The horses got a drink, though, and we stripped our clothes off and rolled around in it, and washed our faces, and that helped some. There was a lot of tule weeds around there, and while we was taking off the pack, I saw a coyote sneak out of the other side of the tule weeds and hit a lope for the hills. The other fellow took a shot at him and knocked him over. We each took a hind quarter of that coyote, and we got some cow chips and made a fire and roasted it. It smelled like carrion. I would take a bite and then retch, and after a while I got just one swallow down.

---

[2] They were traveling with horses only. The normal rate of travel with horses is about forty miles a day, with cattle about ten miles a day.

Riding the Range in '82

We made our beds and went to sleep, figuring that we could make it to the Platte River next day, fifty or sixty miles, and get out of this alive even if somewhat thinner. But at daylight we heard a bell ringing and it woke us up. And a fellow rode up on horseback and wanted to know what the hell we was doing there. When we told him, I thought he'd die laughing. He was out after the horses for the roundup, and he had seen ours and come down there, thinking they were some of his.

They were camped half a mile over the hill, on a bubbling spring.

7

Thorns an Inch Long—
A Homesick Texan—Trail Bosses Knew Their Job—
Lightning and Hail—
"You Can Sleep All Winter When You Get to Montana"

I stayed on the Platte all the summer of '82 with different outfits and made several trips to the railroad with beef herds. In the fall I got paid off and went home to see about my own cattle. I ain't a damn bit proud of that winter, too much wine, women, and song. So in the spring I sold my cattle and drifted south once more.

I hired out in Texas to the F U F outfit, that was run by some people from New England, to take another herd up the trail. And that was the time I went all the way up to the Yellowstone River in Montana, which was the goal of every cowpuncher's ambition in the eighties. They all wanted to get to the Yellowstone.

We started out the tenth day of April, 1883, and we turned them loose on Armell's Creek, near Forsyth, Montana, in October. We put up that herd near San Antone. The trail outfit was hired there, and the different ranches was bringing the cattle in to us in little bunches, and we received them and road-branded them. The country south of San Antone is brush country, South Texas brush, mesquite and cactus and thorn and I don't know what else, but I know everything that grows has thorns on it except the willows, and some of them are an inch long.

Thorns an Inch Long

One night at sundown, after we had been working the cattle in the brush all day, we came to a little open prairie just about big enough to bed down the herd. I tied my night horse to the wagon, took off my chaps and laid down on them, pulled my slicker over me, and went to sleep. About nine o'clock a clap of thunder woke me up, and somebody hollered: "They're running." I grabbed my hat and jumped for my horse, forgetting to put on my chaps, and I spent half the night chasing the cattle through that thorny brush. When daylight come and we got them all together, we hadn't lost a head. But I was a bloody sight. I had a big hole in my forehead, and my face was all over blood, my hands was cut to pieces—because I'd left my gloves in my chaps pocket—and my knees was the worst of all. I was picking thorns out of them all the way to Kansas. That morning I said to the boss: "If God Almighty ever lets me out of this brush, I'm never going back into it." And I never have.

On the other hand there was fellows brought up in the brush that like it and never could feel at home in any other kind of country. Another outfit that came up the trail that year had a little Texas cowboy with them who had never gotten out of the brush. He would start up the trail, but as soon at they got out of the Cross Timbers in the Nations, which was the last piece of timbered country on the trail, this little fellow would stampede back to Texas. He had run away like this three times—leaving the outfit short a hand —and the bunch he was with this time had made up their minds he wouldn't do it to them. So they jumped him one day at noon and hog-tied him and put him in the wagon until after dark, and then they let him out on herd. Next day it was too far to run away, so he stayed and went up the trail. But he said: "You know, when I get out on that big prairie I feel kind of naked."

It was open country all the way up, until he got to Squaw Creek on the Missouri. There is lots of brush and bull pines on Squaw Creek, so when he got there he felt at home, and I heard that in the end he took up land there.

In the eighties, conditions on the trail were a whole lot better than they were in the seventies. Someone had invented mess boxes to set up in the hind end of the wagon; they had four-horse teams to pull it, lots of grub, and from six to eight horses for each man to ride; and the saddles had improved. When I was on the trail in '83, we didn't have hardly a sore-backed horse all the way up to Montana, and the trail bosses had got the handling of a herd down to a science.

After some experience in the business, they found that about 2,000 head on an average was the best number in a herd. After you crossed Red River and got out on the open plains, it was sure a pretty sight to see them strung our for almost a mile, the sun flashing on their horns. At noon you would see the men throw them off the trail, and half the crew would go to dinner while the other half would graze them onto water. No orders were given; every man knew his place and what to do. The left point, right swing, left flank, and right drag would go in to dinner together. The first men off would eat in a hurry, catch up fresh horses, and go out on a lope to the herd. It sure looks good, when you are on herd and hungry, to see the relief come out on a lope.

Eleven men made the average crew with a trail herd. The two men in the lead were called the point men, and then as the herd strung out there would be two men behind them on the swing, two on the flank, and the two drag drivers in the rear. With the cook and horse wrangler and boss, that made eleven. The poorest men always worked with the drags, because a good hand wouldn't stand for it. I have seem them come off herd with the dust half an inch deep on their hats and thick as fur in their eyebrows and mustaches, and if they shook their head or you tapped their cheek, it would fall off them in showers. That dust was the reason a good man wouldn't work back there, and if they hired out to a trail outfit and were put with the drags, they would go to the boss and ask for their time. But the rest of them were pretty nearly as bad off when they were on the side away from the wind. They would go to the water barrel at the end of the day and rinse their mouths and cough and spit and bring up that black stuff out of their throats. But you couldn't get it up out of your lungs.

Going into a new country, the trail boss had to ride his tail off hunting for water. But he would come back to the wagon at night. Lots of times he would ride up on a little knoll and signal to the point—water this way, or water that way. And that is when you will see some trail work, when they are going to turn the herd. If they're going to turn to the right the man on the right point will drop back, and the man on left point will go ahead and start pushing them over, and the men behind can tell from their movements what they want to do. By watching and cutting the curve, you can save the drags two or three hundred yards. It's the drags you have to protect—they are the weak and sore-footed cattle—and that's what counts in the management of a herd.

There is quite an art, too, to watering a herd. You bring them up and spread them out along the bank, with the lead cattle headed downstream. The leads get there first, and of course they drink clear water, and as the drags keep coming in they get clear water, too, because they are upstream.

Oh, those trail bosses know their business, and their business was to get their herd through in good shape; that was all they thought about. Coming up to the mouth of the

63

Musselshell in '84—I had been in Montana a year by that time, but I was going further north with the N Bar herd—we watered one day on a little muddy creek, and they sure roiled it up. That day at dinner my pal Harry Rutter told Burgess, the boss: "Say, you go ahead and water the wagon and horses, and then you water the herd, and then we get a drink. I ain't kicking, but I had to chew that water before I could swallow it."

1883 and 1884 were the biggest years there ever was on the Texas trail. John Blocker says that 500,000 cattle passed through Ogallala alone in those two years, and that was just one point. A lot of the herds going north went to the west of there, while others never got into Nebraska at all, but were shipped east from Dodge City, Kansas. After 1884 the cattle drives began to fall off. In the winter of 1884–85 Kansas passed a quarantine law against Texas cattle on account of Texas fever, and next season the trail had to move west to Trail City, Colorado. In '86 there was a big drive of stock cattle to northern Wyoming and Montana, and a 90 per cent loss that winter, which took the heart out of the business as far as the northern ranges were concerned. From then on the drives got smaller and smaller, till in '95 the X I T Ranch in the Texas Panhandle brought up three herds. And that was the last of the Texas trail.

But in 1883 all the cattle in the world seemed to be coming up from Texas. On the trail we were hardly ever out of sight of a herd, and when we got to that big flat country along the North Platte we could see the dust of the others for twenty miles. One afternoon I was out hunting some of our horses—because we had brought a lot of wild range horses up from Texas with us, and bought more at North Platte, and they were always getting away. And I rode up on a little hill to look for the horses, and from the top of the hill I could see seven herds behind us; I knew there were eight herds ahead of us, and I could see the dust from thirteen more of them on the other side of the river.

On another hill on the north side of the North Platte, near Cold Water, was where I left the herd and lay down in the shade. That was counted a disgrace, but I had been in the saddle two nights and three days.

The first night after we crossed the river with the F U F herd I was on night guard, ten to twelve, and it came up an awful hailstorm. I told my partner, a kid from Boston, to ride to one side and take the saddle off and hold it over his head. And pretty soon I had to quit, too, and hold my saddle over my head, and there were still dents in that saddle when I traded it off in Buffalo, Wyoming, a year later. Nobody knows now what those storms were like, because nobody has to stay out in them any more, but believe me, they were awful. If you had to take that drumming on your head, it would drive you crazy.

I lost my horse that night, because a big hailstone hit my hand, and it hurt so bad I let go the reins as he plunged. The rest of the night I was afoot and helpless. Nobody came out from camp to relieve us, because camp was on the other side of a big coulee—arroyo, they call it down there—and it was swimming water and they couldn't get across. So all that night my partner and I were out there with the herd alone.

The next night another storm came up and, by God, it was my relief again. The second night nobody in the outfit got any sleep, but the rest of them only had one night of it, and my partner and I had two. Five herds was camped close together when that storm struck, and next day 10,000 range cattle was all mixed up. We rounded up and cut our cattle out; it was hot as hell, and in that country along the Platte there wasn't a tree nor even any brush for fifty or sixty miles.

65

About three in the afternoon, on Cold Water Creek, I saw a sod house that some cow outfit had built there for a line camp, and I saw where this little bit of a house made a patch of shade. So I rode over to it, and got off my horse and I took my rope down and laid on it, so the horse couldn't leave me. And I just died.

When I woke up, it was dark. I could see our campfire away up the flat. I rode out there and asked the boss to figure out what he owed me, because I thought I would get fired for quitting the herd and I wanted to beat him to it.

But all he said was: "Hell, Ted, I thought you was going to do that yesterday."

They used to have some terrible storms on the North and South Platte. The year before this, in '82, I was in one that killed fourteen head of cattle and six or seven horses and two men, on the different herds. One man was so scared he threw his six-shooter away, for fear it would draw the lightning; and I remember old Matt Winter, with the rain apouring down and the lightning flashing, taking off his hat and yelling at God Almighty: "All right, you old bald-headed son of a bitch up there, if you want to kill me, come on do it!" It scared the daylights out of the rest of us.

Lots of cowpunchers were killed by lightning, and that is history. I was knocked off my horse by it twice. The first time I saw a ball of fire coming toward me and felt something strike me on the head. When I came to, I was lying under old Pete and the rain was pouring down on my face. The second time I was trying to get under a railroad bridge when it hit me, and I came to in the ditch. The cattle were always restless when there was a storm at night, even if it was a long way off, and that was when any little thing would start a run. Lots of times I have ridden around the herd, with lightning playing and thunder muttering in the distance, when the air was so full of electricity that I would see it flashing on the horns of the cattle, and there would be balls of it on the horse's ears and even on my mustache, little balls about the size of a pea. I suppose it was static electricity, the same as when you shake a blanket on a winter night in a dark room.

But when you add it all up, I believe the worst hardship we had on the trail was loss of sleep. There was never enough sleep. Our day wouldn't end till about nine o'clock, when we grazed the herd onto the bed ground. And after that every man in the outfit except the boss and horse wrangler and cook would have to stand two hours' night guard. Suppose my guard was twelve to two. I would stake my night horse, unroll my bed, pull off my boots, and crawl in at nine, get about three hours' sleep, and then ride two hours. Then I would come off guard and get to sleep another hour and a half, till the cook yelled, "Roll out," at half past three. So I would get maybe five hours' sleep when the weather was nice and everything smooth and pretty, with cowboys singing under the stars. If it wasn't so nice, you'd be lucky to sleep an hour. But the wagon rolled on in the morning just the same.

That night guard got to be part of our lives. They never had to call me. I would hear the fellow coming off herd—because laying with your ear to the ground you could hear that horse trotting a mile off—and I would jump up and put my hat and boots on and go out to meet him. We were all just the same. I remember when we got up to the mouth of the Musselshell in '84 we turned them loose, and Johnny Burgess, the trail boss, said: "We won't stand no guard tonight, boys," and it sounded good. But every man in that outfit woke when his time to go on guard came, and looked around and wanted to know why they didn't call him.

67

Sometimes we would rub tobacco juice in our eyes to keep awake. It was rubbing them with fire. I have done that a few times, and I have often sat in my saddle sound asleep for just a few minutes. In '79, when we hit the Platte River with that Olive herd, a strong north wind was blowing waves two feet high in their faces, and they bulled on us, which means they won't do nothing, only stand and look at you. So since they wouldn't take the water we had to hold them, and we had one of those bad electric storms and they run nearly all night. We got them across the river the next day, and that night on guard my partner, Joe Buckner, says: "Teddy, I am going to Greenland where the nights are six months long, and I ain't agoing to get up until ten o'clock next day."

But if you said anything to the boss, he would only say: "What the hell are you kicking about? You can sleep all winter when you get to Montana."

8

On the Trail in '83—Theft of a Pillow—
Giving the U. P. Passengers a Thrill—
A Pious New Englander—
Calamity Jane Gets Us a Drink—I Repay a Debt

One little thing that happened when we were coming up in '83 would have made another picture for Charlie Russell. Going across Kansas, we went right through a little town of ten or fifteen houses, that was built up alongside the trail. And as another fellow and I rode through there with the herd, we looked in the window of a little house on the edge of town, and inside the open window we saw two big, white pillows on a bed, that I suppose some settler's wife was awful proud of, though I never thought of that at the time. I said, "Here's where I sleep soft from now on," and I leaned down from my horse and grabbed one of the pillows and he took the other, and we throwed them in the wagon. I still had mine when I was married.

It was a dirty trick as I look at it now, but there was no love lost between settlers and cowboys on the trail. Those jayhawkers would take up a claim right where the herds watered and charge us for water. They would plant a crop alongside the trail and plow a furrow around it for a fence, and then when the cattle got into their wheat or their garden patch, they would come out cussing and waving a shotgun and yelling for damages. And the cattle had been coming through there when they were still raising punkins in Illinois.

69

After we got up to Fort Kearney in '83 with the F U F herd, the outfit bought a whole lot more cattle and horses in Kansas and Missouri and brought them all together at Fort Kearney. I went back down into Kansas to help bring up another six hundred head, and that is a trip that I never want to repeat. There were four of us, and we had one horse apiece, with one man driving the wagon—because while the outfit had been buying horses all the way, they didn't have enough broke horses, and were too busy to break them and too damn stingy to buy any. And that was the way we was supposed to take those six hundred head of cattle two hundred miles. For two solid days we was going through fall wheat that was a foot high on each side of the narrow road, and no fence; and we all rode the tails off our one horse apiece, trying to keep the cattle out of it. But it was no use. They was grazing the wheat all the way, and we kept paying, paying, paying till the money was all gone, and then we sold a couple of cows.

When we were going through the last wheat field, the road followed the Kansas-Nebraska line for quite a ways before turning north, and while we were still on the line, I saw the sheriff coming after us. You could see the sun shining on that star of his a long way off. So we fogged them across the line into Nebraska, and when we got them over there, we held them down in a coulee. My horse was just about all in, and if he hadn't been a grain-fed horse, he never would have stood up. Pretty soon the sheriff showed up and begun talking like he was going to collect a fine, but we pointed out that we was in Nebraska, and he shut up because he knew he couldn't do a thing. And where we were then, at Wymore, Nebraska, we had 145 miles ahead of us yet, all wheat fields. And I said to the boss: "Tell that old Yankee that's running this outfit to bring a string of cars down here and get these cattle of his on the train." If he hadn't, I'd have quit and so would the rest of us.

We pulled out of Fort Kearney with the main herd in August, 1883. The States cattle that had been shipped in were very poor and the grass was good along the Platte, so we just drifted along slow and let them graze, and as the boys did not have to work much, they got to feeling gay. We were following up the U. P. Railroad and the emigrant trains were full of people going West, so we thought we would give them a thrill. One day we made a dummy man stuffed with grass, put a rope around his neck, and threw the other end over the crossbar of a telegraph pole. Just as the train pulled in, I yanked him up by the rope around my saddle horn, and the whole outfit began to shoot at him as he swung in the air. They shot the rope in two and down he came; someone handed me the rope, and away I went on a dead run across the flat, dragging him, the whole outfit right after me, shooting, as he bounced along. The people on the train were scared to death. Women fainted and chil-

dren screamed. They begged the conductor to pull out before we held up the train. Somebody even telegraphed to Lincoln saying the F U F cowboys had hung a horse thief.

Hell began to pop. Here come the boss on the next train, just foaming; here come a spring wagon loaded with the sheriff and coroner. My old boss Marion Olive was driving the team—he run a livery stable at Plum Creek. He says to me: "Keep your mouth shut, Ted"—thinking it was on the square. The sheriff demanded the corpse at once. We pointed to it and they drove up. I can hear yet how Marion Olive laughed when they turned it over.

Well, it ended in a big laugh all around, but our fun was finished. The old man made us hit the trail in earnest for Montana.

The manager and part-owner of the F U F was an old man named Fuller,[1] from Vermont, and what he didn't know about a trail herd would make a book so big you couldn't load it on a flatcar with a block and tackle. He had fed a lot of cattle in Nebraska on corn, but he didn't know a cowpuncher when he saw one, and he hired everybody who come along. There was only three or four good hands in the outfit, counting myself as one. The rest of them didn't know enough to pull on a rope. I remember there was an Englishman named Biggs, whose father was some kind of a titled high-up; there was the nephew of the president of the company, from Vermont, and a Frenchman from Louisiana who always went to sleep on night herd. I had to show them everything. I was getting seventy-five dollars a month, and they even put me in charge of a wagon for awhile, coming through them wheat fields. But I couldn't handle men. The boss had to sit still and look wise, and I never was any good at that.

[1] Fictitious name.

In spite of the good pay I didn't like that outfit; you couldn't like it, the way it was run. Half the orders Fuller gave us was all wrong, and that's the hardest kind of a job, to do something when you know it is wrong. A man like that had no business trying to run a cow outfit. He didn't know nothing and he couldn't get along with cowpunchers. He was one of these pious New Englanders, that would say his prayers at night and then give you ten dollars to steal a calf the next day.

And I can tell you more than that about what his religion was like. When we were putting up the herd at Fort Kearney, we bought a lot of horses and cattle in Missouri and took them to Fort Kearney by train, and I went down there to help bring them up. We had a couple of trainloads, and the first train was mostly horses. By order of Mr. Fuller all the cars was bedded with straw instead of sand—because it was cheaper, I suppose. And going uphill against the wind the sparks from the engine set the front car on fire. We didn't discover it for quite awhile, back there in the caboose, and when we did see it we couldn't get the engineer to stop. I was running along over the top of the train toward the engine, shooting at the bell with my six-shooter, and he caught on that something was wrong finally and we got them out as fast as we could. But it was too late. Those horses— oh, God, I never want to see anything like that again. Some of them was still alive. Their eyes burned out, and all their hair was gone, and blood was coming out of their nostrils with every breath. We was going to shoot them, but that old man wouldn't let us. He said if we did he might not be able to collect his damages from the railroad company. So we went off and left them there. The man in charge of the second train shot them when he came along.

Although Mr. Fuller didn't know one end of a cow from

the other, that didn't stop him from trying to revolutionize the cowboys. He told us down on the Platte that those was his intentions, and when we got up to the Yellowstone he went to work to carry them out. He issued orders forbidding us to bring the *Police Gazette* to the ranch. And when we went to town we were not to take a drink, and he went along to see that the order was obeyed. We couldn't do nothing but give in to him, more or less. We were strangers up north, and winter was coming on. We were getting big wages. We had to take a tumble.

Along toward the end of that fall the outfit was all in Miles City. One day the old man was sitting in the hotel lobby, where he could keep his eye on the bar and see that none of his boys was in there, when in walked Calamity Jane. The first time I ever saw her was five years before this, in the Black Hills in '78, when I went up there from the Platte River with that beef herd. I didn't meet her then, but I got a good look at her, when she was at the height of her fame and looks. I remember she was dressed in purple velvet, with diamonds on her and everything. As I recall it, she was some sort of a madam at that time, running a great big gambling hall in Deadwood.

In Miles City in the fall of '83, I had met her and bought her a few drinks. We knew a lot of the same people. So when she came into the hotel lobby where old man Fuller was, I went over and told her about him, and I said: "I'll give you two dollars and a half if you'll go and sit on his lap and kiss him."

And she was game. She walked up to him with everybody watching her, and sat down on his lap, and throwed both her arms around him so his arms were pinned to his sides and he couldn't help himself—she was strong as a bear. And then she began kissing him and saying: "Why don't you ever come to see me any more, honey? You know I love you." And so forth.

I told him: "Go ahead. Have a good time. It's customary here. I won't write home and tell your folks about it."

The old man spluttered and spit and wiped his mouth on his handkerchief. And he left the hotel and that was the last we saw of him that night.

Later that winter I met Calamity Jane again at Belly-Ups stage station, which was the first station out of Miles City on the Miles-Deadwood stage line. They named it that in honor of the buffalo hunters, who all went belly-ups in the winter of '83 because the buffalo was all gone. Anyway, I met her there, and I borrowed fifty cents from her to buy a meal. I wasn't broke, because I had plenty of money at the ranch, but I had blowed all I had with me, so it come to the same thing.

I thanked her for the fifty cents and said: "Some day I'll pay you." And she said: "I don't give a damn if you never pay me." She meant it, because she was always the kind that would share her last cent.

And I never saw her again until twenty-four years later. It was in 1907, and she was standing on a street corner in Gilt Edge; which was more of a town then than it is now, since they took half the buildings away. I walked up to her and said: "Don't you know me?" and gave her the fifty cents. She recognized me then and said: "I told you, Blue, that I didn't give a damn if you never paid me," and we went and drank it up. She had been famous a long time then, traveling with Buffalo Bill's show and so on, and she was getting old. A few years before I met her in Gilt Edge some friends of hers had taken up a collection and sent her East to make a lady of her, and now she was back. I joked her about her trip and asked her: "How'd you like it when they sent you East to get reformed and civilized?"

Her eyes filled with tears. She said: "Blue, why don't the sons of bitches leave me alone and let me go to hell my own route? All I ask is to be allowed to live out the rest of my life with you boys who speak my language. And I hope they lay me beside Bill Hickok when I die."

9

Montana at Last—
An Invitation to the Parsonage—
I Get the Name of "Blue"—Death in a Hotel Room

Coming up in '83, we left the North Platte at Sidney Bridge. Frank Abbott was our trail boss up to that point, but then he went up to Idaho for some more horses, and a fellow named Veto Cross took us on up to the Yellowstone. From the time we left Fort Kearney we was following the old Oregon trail till we got to Sidney Bridge. It was still plain as could be, and they say is so today in some places, and where the rain had washed out the old ruts it would be up to your saddle skirts.

The outfit was going to locate on Armall's Creek, eight miles south of the town of Forsyth, Montana. We reached there in October, 1883, but I never got to see the Yellowstone River until six weeks later, and the last day on the trail I rode in the wagon, sick from drinking alkali water. The head of the company was waiting for us, and when we got in Mr. Fuller paid off the trail boss and most of the men, and run the outfit himself until Frank Abbott got in with the horses from Idaho.

There was nothing there at all, only sagebrush, when we arrived. Buildings and corrals all had to be built, but the cowpunchers didn't do any of it. They had an outfit just to do that work, and we lived in tents until they was finished.

We was busy riding all day and every day, keeping the horses and cattle from straying on their new range. The house was made of logs, but they weren't squared off nice, the way you see them now, just throwed together and the ends left sticking out. Inside there was bunks to sleep on, benches to sit on, and a homemade table, and that was all.

I paid a visit to Forsyth about a year ago, and the people there were talking to me about "old-timers" who come into the country in the late nineties, or even as late as 1910. When our outfit got up there in the fall of '83, Forsyth had a store, two saloons, a barber shop, a livery stable, and a hotel that was closed up—the buffalo hunters having quit. The only women in the town were the storekeeper's wife, and a fat old haybag who had been scalped by Indians at the mouth of the Musselshell a few years before, and was laying up with the barber. She had another one of those nicknames you can't repeat, much less print it. What there was of the town was strung out along one side of the railroad track the way it is today, only they have a nice park there now. The Northern Pacific was completed through Montana that year, and President Arthur took a trip over the line to celebrate it. I remember when I went down to Forsyth to shoe a horse that fall, somebody said, "The President's coming through here on the train." So I waited to see it, and it came through all decorated with flags.

The old man was dead in earnest about reforming this cowboy business. The night we got up there with the cattle he had a Presbyterian preacher and his daughter on hand to convert us. They had come up from Miles City at the old man's invitation, so we drug out some logs to sit on, and built a fire in the middle, and held a revival meeting, with the preacher preaching salvation and the girl leading the hymns.

78

I Get the Name of "Blue"

She was a pretty girl, about nineteen years old, and we were all strong for religion. I liked to sing and had a good voice, so I was away out front when it came to "Pull for the Shore" and the other revival hymns. After it was over, the girl came up to a couple of us who had shown the most religious spirit and invited us to make the parsonage our home when we came to Miles City, so we could stay out of temptation.

You know what kind of temptation she was trying to keep us out of, and what chance she had—hot-blooded young fellows who hadn't seen a woman, hardly, for six months. But of course we said yes, and she went back to Miles City real pleased at having made a couple of converts. A friend of mine, Billy Smith the stock inspector, lived next door to the parsonage, and she even boasted to him about how she had reformed me. He said: "Reformed Ted? Why, he's the wildest cowpuncher in Montana."

After that revival meeting I rode the range for several weeks with a pack outfit, looking for horses we had lost on the way up here—those wild range horses was giving us trouble all the way. I rode clear down through the Crow Reservation country, almost to Sheridan, and it wasn't until late fall that I got to Miles City. The morning after I got there, or it might have been afternoon, I had just been having breakfast with a girl, and I was walking down the street beside her, feeling awful good and singing my favorite song:

The little black bull come down the mountain
(Hoorah Johnny and a hoorah Johnny) . . .

but I will tell about that song later. And who should we meet but the blue-eyed Presbyterian girl. When she saw

79

the company I was with, if looks could kill, the look she give me would have sure done it. But she made one last effort to save my soul.

"Remember, Mr. Abbott," she said, "if you should ever change your mind, there will always be a room for you at the parsonage."

Billy Smith was standing across the street in the door of the Sideboard Saloon, watching us, and he burst out laughing. He said: "Ain't that hell! The girls beat her to it."

And that story will follow me all the rest of my days. In 1934 I went to the stock convention at Miles City, fifty-one years after this thing happened, and I didn't like my room at the hotel and asked the clerk if I could change it. He said: "I'm sorry, Mr. Abbott, we haven't another room, but I understand there's a room for you at the Presbyterian parsonage."

It was the night before I met the preacher's daughter that I got the name of Blue, and that is another thing I will never be rid of. There was a theatre in Miles City, Turner's Theatre, it was called, and I went in there that night, and one of these box rustlers came up to me. You know in that kind of theatres they used to have curtained boxes running all around inside, and box rustlers was what they called the girls that worked them. So this girl came up to me and she had on a little skirt, like a circus girl, and tights that looked like she had been melted and run into them. And first she invited me upstairs to buy wine—at five dollars a bottle. I said nothing doing to that. And then she told me she had a room back there and invited me to go with her. That sounded better to me and I was going to go. But there was a dark hall that ran around behind the stage, and as we started along it I remembered that I had seven hundred dollars on me, in my six-shooter belt. Part of it was left over

*Teddy Blue, John Burgess, and John Bowen
in Miles City, 1884*

Granville Stuart and his first wife

from that money I inherited, and besides I was drawing top hand's wages, seventy-five dollars a month, and I had all that money too. And I thought there might be some kind of a deadfall back there—I was a wise guy—I'd heard those stories.

So I turned around, and as I turned my spur catched on a carpet and I fell through a thin partition onto the stage. Well, I thought, if you're before an audience you've got to do something, so I grabbed a chair from one of the musicians and straddled it and bucked it all around the stage, yelling, "Whoa, Blue! Whoa, Blue!"—which was a cowpuncher expression at that time. Before they even got me off the stage, it had started. The manager yelled, "Hey, Blue, come out of there," and the audience was yelling with laughter and they took it up. And when I went out of that theatre that night I was Blue, and Teddy Blue I have been for fifty-five years.

I was in Miles City a second time that fall, and that time one of the boys with the outfit got sick, and I nursed him in a hotel room until he died in my arms. He was not a real cowboy. He had been a bookkeeper for the president of the company in St. Paul, and he came out to Montana for his health. He had t.b., bad. He had been at the ranch a few months when he got so sick the old man brought him in town and left him there, and he said to the rest of us: "One of you ought to stay with him." He looked right at me, and I said I would stay.

He only lived a week, but that week in that hotel room was the worst I ever went through. He kept having hemorrhages, blood all over everything, and I took newspapers and spread them on the bedclothes and on the floor. He did not want me to leave him a minute. We were just two boys in a strange land, but the people at the hotel were as kind as could be. They all offered to do anything they could to help, two ladies especially. One was Mrs. Malone, whose husband came out to Montana with the railroad and then went into the cattle business; she would always do anything for the cowboys. The other was Mrs. Walt Alderson[1] from Tongue River, who I understand is now living at a dude ranch in Wyoming. She was a beautiful young lady in '83, and I sure hope the sun shines on her all the rest of her life. The two of them came up to the room every day, and fixed things up and offered their sympathy.

After I had been there with the kid a week, Mr. Fuller came down one night to see him and he told me: "You'd better go to bed." I hadn't been to bed all that time, only slept in chair once in awhile, because he wouldn't sleep unless he could lay his head on my arm. So I went and laid down in another room. About midnight Mr. Fuller come for me and said: "You'd better come now. He's asking for you." I guess he knew he was going. So I went back where he was, and he wanted to know if I would lay down beside him and let him rest his head on my shoulder. In a few minutes he mumbled something about Ethel, his sister I think, and then he was gone.

It put me right up in the air. I went down to the bar to get a drink. There was a captain there that I knew, from Fort Keogh. He was dressed in civilian clothes, with a hard hat on, and he took his hat off and his coat off and gave them to me and said: "You go for a walk and get some fresh air." So I went out, but I went to a honky-tonk the first damn thing—trying to get it off my mind.

They shipped him out next day to Boston.

[1] Mother of Mrs. Bill Eaton of Eaton's ranch.

10

Another Seagoing Yankee—
I Go to Work for the N Bar—Repping in '84—
"Forty Years a Cowpuncher"—
"The Best-Looking Cowboy on Powder River"

Just before Christmas we had a hell of a row at the F U F and all quit, and that was when we went to Miles City the second time. The old man had ordered us not to kill any beef. We was supposed to live on that old condemned sow-belly he'd bought from Fort Keogh, that even the soldiers wouldn't eat. But our wagon boss, Frank Abbott, killed a beef anyway and cached it in a haystack, and when the building crew came up to put up some more buildings, he thought they was working hard, cutting down trees and so on, so he gave them some of it. The old man heard of it and called us on the carpet, and we all threw up our jobs. But it blew over. The outfit needed us, and we couldn't afford to be out of jobs in the dead of winter. So we kind of made up in Miles City, when that boy died.

But in April I quit the F U F for good and went to work for Matt Winters, who was in Montana now like the rest of us, running an outfit on Otter Creek for T. J. Bryan, the first head of the Montana Stock Association. Right after I went to work for him I helped receive a trainload of Iowa cattle at Miles City. Before we could take them out to Otter Creek there was a terrible blizzard, and we lost two hundred head of them right in the stockyards. They had just come off the train and they were weak.

I didn't stay with Matt, either, very long. We started in on the roundup, and he put me to work riding for Cap' Howe, who had an outfit up Otter Creek from the Bryan outfit. And Cap' Howe sent me over a string of damn bum horses. Anybody knows what that means who has ever tried to rope calves on a fool horse that doesn't know his business. It's enough to drive you crazy. But old Cap' Howe was another of these seagoing Yankees in the cattle business—to his mind a horse was just a horse and you had to ride him.

Still, there's ways of getting rid of a horse you don't like, and I sure got rid of one of them broomtails—the most worthless damn horse I ever saw in my life. He was a mean, ornery devil in the first place, that would pull back on you every time you'd go to get on, or rear up and try to kill you. And he was absolutely useless when you got him in a herd. I was trying to use him for a cutting horse, and the balky fool would bull on me in the midst of the cattle and I couldn't even move him. Nobody can work on a horse like that.

So one morning when I was saddling him I tied him with a long rope to the top corral pole. You know the top pole is loose; they just rest it on the uprights. And when I went to put on the saddle blanket I flapped it in his face, accidentally, you might say, and he reared back like I knew he would and jerked the pole off. And it broke his leg, and they had to shoot him.

As soon as the Otter Creek roundup was over that spring, I left Matt and went to work for the N Bar outfit, and I stayed with them a year. The N Bar—Niobrara Cattle Company—was owned by the Newman Brothers of St. Louis, and was one of the big early outfits that made history on the range. It started out as an Indian contract outfit down in Nebraska, buying trail herds in Ogallala and delivering them for beef to the Indian agencies. Then in '79 New-man Brothers began running cattle themselves on the Nio-brara River at Boiling Springs, Nebraska; and in '82 they branched out with a second outfit on Powder River, in Wyoming. In '84, they trailed two herds of 2,000 Texas steers each all the way up to the mouth of the Musselshell River, one hundred miles or so north of the Yellowstone, and started in to run that as a third outfit.

Zeke Newman was one of the greatest men that ever was in the cattle business, and the kind of a boss that cowpunch-ers understood and respected. His brother, H. L., was the head of that firm, and he was a banker, but Zeke Newman, Uncle Zeke we called him, was the cowman. Zeke was a great gambler. He used to run a freight outfit up in Mon-tana in the sixties. They say that one time in Helena—it was the seventies by that time, and Zeke Newman had sold his bull outfit and was quitting the country—he had $30,000 on him in cash, and he got in a faro game and started to buck the bank, and he lost $20,000 of it. So he said: "Hell, I might as well be broke," and he put the other $10,000 down on one turn. And he won and he went out of there with $40,000. I wasn't there to see this, you understand, but it's what the boys told me.

Like so many of those old-time cattlemen he was a big spender and very liberal. He had a wagon boss named Harry Landers—the same Landers that lost his herd on Green River that time—and Newman thought so much of him that he gave him a forty-five-dollar single-action six-shooter with an ivory handle, and an N Bar in gold set in it. Every-body thought a lot of Zeke, because if you got into trouble or got broke or sick or anything, he would let you have money and would see you through. But he expected abso-lute loyalty in return. And he sure as hell got it. He was a good man for cowpunchers to work for, but he wasn't as good as Granville Stuart. Because Granville Stuart would do everything Zeke Newman did for you and let you own cattle, too. Zeke Newman wouldn't let you own a head—for all the friendship between him and Harry Landers, he fired him on account of it.

That summer of '84 I went to all the roundups as a rep for the N Bar. The word rep was short for representative— no cowpuncher could remember a long word like that. On the open range each big outfit, or bunch of little ones, besides working on the roundup in their own territory, would send a rep to the neighboring roundups to gather up stray cattle. You would be out all summer that way, because it takes them a good many weeks to brand the calves, and when that is all done about midsummer, they will knock off, maybe, for a week or two. And then they will start in and gather the beef, and they keep at that until way late in the fall.

The whole thing was run according to a system. By '84 the range in southern Montana and Wyoming was all organized into roundup districts, bounded by certain mountain ranges and streams. There were no fences, and while each outfit would have a line that it called the boundary of its own range, the cattle drifted, and they all ran together more or less. All the outfits belonging to any one roundup would get together in the spring with their wagons and work through the territory, creek by creek. Ownership of a calf was determined by the brand on the cow. A maverick was a big calf that had been missed in a roundup and gotten weaned away from its mother before it had any brand, so there was no way of telling who owned it, but that did not prevent a lot of people from using a rope and a running iron for their own benefit.

The cowpunchers all liked repping. A rep traveled with

a big string of horses, and he was a notch higher than a common cowboy. He had to be, to keep all those different brands and marks in his head. Not all of them could do that, but I always could. As soon as I saw a cow, I knew what out-fit owned her, clear down to the Platte. If you start in as a kid and don't do but one thing all your life, you're bound to get your head full of it, especially if you like what you're doing. Another thing about repping was, it gave you a chance to go to all the different roundups and the roundup was something everybody looked forward to, on the range. You got to see a lot of people that way and hear all the news. Cowpunchers was alone so much, that was why they ap-preciated company.

But the biggest thing about repping was that you were on your own instead of working for a boss. For months on end you never even saw him, and they all liked that. At the worst there was never very much bossing done around a cow outfit, but any at all was too much to suit the average cowpuncher.

I wrote "Forty Years a Cowpuncher" that fall while I was repping on the beef roundup on Powder River. That was a song I made up, only it was really a parody on "Jerry, Go an' Ile That Car," which was a railroad song they were singing in the eighties, and it had much the same tune.[1] I made Larry Wolverton the hero of it because his name fitted; he was a top hand for the Scott and Hanks cow out-fit on Powder River. I worked it all out in my head, mostly on herd at night, and that fall in Miles City the boys would buy me a drink for every verse if I would sing it to them. I could always sing. When I was a small boy, I used to stand on a chair beside my mother while she played the piano and sang with me: "Kitty Tyrrell" was the first tune she

1 See page 231.

Teddy Blue's Country

learned me. I sang in school. I was always singing on herd, day or night.

I got to Miles City in the summer of '84, because I was hurt on the roundup. Going out after the horses one morning, my horse reared up and fell on me and I struck my back on a log. So while the rest of them was working hard, I went to town at the company's expense, for rest and medical treatment. After I had been there eight days, Zeke Newman come in town. And he said, "A man who can drink sixty-five dollars worth of whisky while he is eating sixteen dollars' worth of grub is well enough to work," and he ordered me back to the ranch.

But I was still ahead of the game, because I had those eight days in Miles City, and I sure made the most of them. I can never forget Miles City in '84. As far as fun went, I think I had more of it then than any other year of my life, much more fun than when I was a kid, because when I was a kid I was too much on the fight all the time. It was that same old foolishness of worrying about personal courage. When I was eighteen or nineteen I was so full of that shooting business I couldn't be free to enjoy myself, anyway not like I did later. But by the time I was twenty-three I had got over the worst of it and oh, boy, but life was good.

In Miles City that summer I found a lot of new friends and some old ones. There was girls there that I had seen at a lot of different places along the trail. They followed the trail herds. The madams would bring them out from Omaha and Chicago and St. Paul; you would see them in Ogallala, and then again in Cheyenne or the Black Hills. But when the herds was all gone and the beef was shipped, the town was dead. The girls would go back where they came from and the gamblers would go with them. When our outfit came down to Miles City in the fall of '83, there was some new girls there, too, fresh from the East, and they was afraid of us wild Texas cowpunchers; they didn't want to have anything to do with us at first. But they got over that.

Those were the days when I didn't have a care in the world. I had plenty of good horses to ride, and the girls said I was the best-looking cowboy on Powder River. And they cleaned me down to my spurs.

I Quit the Roundup—
Crossing the Yellowstone—"How Far Is It up No'th?"—
I Have Too Much Snap

I quit the beef roundup before they were finished that fall, because I had a chance to go down on Powder River and meet those two N Bar trail herds that was coming up from Texas. I went down first to the N Bar ranch on Powder River, at the mouth of Cash Creek, and they got there just as I was packing my bed on a horse to go and meet them. John Burgess was in charge of the first herd and John Bowen of the second; I had knowed them both before this, in Ogallala or on the trail. They came over to the ranch, and Newman was there, and that was the only time I ever remember of the tables being turned on Newman. He was always making some crack about cowpunchers having an easy time—because he was raised in Missouri where they plowed corn afoot, and he thought that was the only kind of work that counted. He commenced grumbling about how much this Montana outfit of his was costing him, and he said: "In Texas you fellows ride two or three horses, and you work for twenty-five or thirty dollars a month, and you eat what they've got in the wagon. As soon as you get to Montana you expect to ride ten horses, have pie three times a day and sleep with the boss."

John Bowen said: "That's all right, Mr. Newman, we work twenty-six hours a day."

Newman thought he had him there and he said: "You damn fool, don't you know there's only twenty-four hours in a day?"

Bowen said: "I know, but we stand night guard two hours every night."

Old Newman roared out to Billie Irvine: "Hitch up that team! I'm going back to Miles City before these damn fools drive me crazy."

The rest of the cowpunchers couldn't understand why I would quit a good string of horses on the roundup to go with a trail herd. But I wanted to do it because they was going three hundred miles further up north, and that was what appealed to me. It was all new country up there and I wanted to see it, and anyway this other, in Wyoming and southern Montana, was getting settled up. There was ranches every few miles.

I met them at the crossing of Powder River, like I told you, and went on up with them. Ten days later we got to the Yellowstone, which has drowned more cattle and men than any other river on the Texas trail. The Yellowstone doesn't look like much of a river because it is narrow, but it is fast and awful cold, and it has an undercurrent. When we got to the bank, we stopped to loosen our cinches, getting ready to cross, and I took my clothes off. The other men with the outfit said: "What are you taking your clothes off for? Hell, it's nothing but a crick." One man wouldn't even take off his boots. He said: "I'm not agoing to take my boots off to cross no crick." I told them: "You'll think it's the Atlantic Ocean before you've got to the other side."

We crossed at Fort Keogh, which is right next to Miles City, sending the wagons over on the ferry. The danger of swimming rivers is that the cattle will get to milling, and the first thing you know they will start to jump up and ride

91

one another, trying to climb out, and down they will go and you will lose a lot of them. You have to keep them pointed for the opposite bank, which means that in the water each man has to hold his place alongside the herd, just like on the trail.

It was cold, and there was a lot of new ice along the banks, what we call mush ice. When we took the water, I was all right, because I was riding a big Oregon horse named Jesse, that kept his tail right up and wouldn't let the water run over the saddle. But the other men had a tough time. I can see those little Texas horses, with their heads in the air and all the rest of them under the water—because the damn little stinkers will keep reaching for the bottom with their hind feet, so it's all you can do to keep from being drowned off their backs. One man, as soon as that cold water struck his belly, gave a yell and dove off over his horse's head, and he was near drowning. Somebody yelled: "Grab a steer by the tail," and he did, and he never let go until the steer dragged him halfway up the bank, and it took all the skin off his knees.

When we got to the other side they were all sitting on their horses, shivering, with the water running off them, and a fellow said: "That's colder than any ice water I ever drank in Texas." He was a south Texas brush popper who had never been north before. All the way up, after I struck them, he kept asking: "How far is it up no'th?"—as though "up no'th" was a place on the map. I asked him how far he'd ever been up north. He said: "I been no'th clear to San Antone." Then he wanted to know: "Is it cold up no'th?" and I told him: "Colder than you've ever seen it." He said: "Oh, I've seen ice half an inch thick." He was like a lot of those Texas fellows—put him afoot and he didn't know a thing. But he held the right point of that herd all the way from the Guadaloupe River to the mouth of the Musselshell. He was Cow—one of the best cowhands I ever saw.

After we got across the Yellowstone they furnished us a Frenchman named Nado, an old American Fur Company man, to pilot us in. He was supposed to show us where the water was and save us a lot of riding. But we'd have been better off without him. He thought water for four horses was water enough for us, with our 150 head of horses and two full herds of better than 2,000 head in each. He'd been over the country with a couple of pack horses, and that was the limit to his ideas. The year before, when I was with the F U F herd, we had another of those old fellows for a pilot, an old army bullwhacker and mule skinner by the name of Buckskin Joe, who had been in that country for years before the cowmen ever got there. We was curious about "up no'th" ourselves, so we was asking him all kinds of questions. "What kind of a climate is it in Montana?" we asked him, and he give the best answer I ever heard. "I'll tell you what kind of a climate it is. You want a buffalo overcoat, a linen duster, and a slicker with you all the time."

When Nado was finding our water for us was when I saw Burgess and Harry Rutter water 2,000 head of cattle at Skunk Springs. The springs was about as big as a wagon box, and if those big beeves had been allowed to crowd in there, they would have trampled it into a mudhole in a few minutes. But they brought them up to it easy and as they grazed around they'd cut them off in little bunches and water them a few at a time. It was the slickest piece of cow work I ever saw in my life—but of course if they'd been dry, nothing would have held them.

From the time we left Miles City we never saw a ranch till we got to Black Butte, at the west end of our range.

There were a few half-breed houses, deserted, on the upper Musselshell, and that was all. It was a cowman's paradise— big grass, all kinds of game except buffalo, and we had it all to ourselves.

It seems as though an awful lot happened to me in the year 1884. And not just to me. It was the same with all of us. About a year ago I saw Harry Rutter, when him and me was the only ones left alive of the men that went up with those two N Bar herds to the mouth of the Musselshell. And it wasn't thirty seconds before we was back at Miles City in '84, talking about the time we left the herd and went to town on a sneak.

After we had swum the Yellowstone, we laid off a day to rest up, on Sunday Creek. We were only a few miles away from Miles City, and after dinner Rutter and I caught up our horses and went in town. Whenever you lay over a day like that, or any time you are holding the herd, it's day on and day off; in other words, half the crew is off and the other half stays with the herd. It was supposed to be our day on, but we went to town anyway.

I took Rutter and introduced him around, and I went to see my own sweetie. And after awhile he said: "I'm going back to camp and get some more money." But I didn't need any more money, because I had lots of friends in Miles City and worlds of credit by that time, so I said I'd stay there and wait for him. After Rutter got back out to camp, he went to sleep, and Burgess sent a fellow named Mesquite Bill in to get me. But I wouldn't leave.

That night about ten or eleven o'clock I drifted into the MacQueen House, and Zeke Newman was in there, playing billiards. The boys had told me a story about Uncle Zeke and something that happened when the outfit was in Ogallala, on their way up here. They had been to town and was all ready to pull out on the trail again, and old Newman handed $500 in bills to Burgess to pay their expenses. And then, he was so drunk, he sat down. And they said he just sat there, and pulled his beard and said: "A man that won't take a drink of whisky doesn't have no snap." They were laughing all the way up the trail about it.

When Uncle Zeke saw me at the MacQueen House, he said to me: "Teddy, what guard are you standing tonight?" —which was a hint that I ought to be out with the herd.

I said: "I give it up."

He said: "Haven't you been drinking?"

I said: "Mr. Newman, the boys told me you said in Ogallaly that a man that wouldn't take a drink didn't have no snap."

He said: "You have too much snap."

And next day Johnny Burgess came in town and fired me. I said: "All right. Give me fifty cents to cross the ferry and I'll get my bed." So he gave it to me, but we went up first and got a couple of drinks, and pretty soon he said: "Hell, I done worse than that myself. Go on out to the herd."

And that was all there was to that. He did fire me later, in earnest. But I never was out of work except that way— on account of some foolishness. If I say it myself, I was a hell of a good cowhand. After we got up to the mouth of the Musselshell that fall, Newman asked Johnny Burgess who he was keeping on for the winter and Burgess, starting to name them, said, "Teddy Blue." Newman said, "What are you keeping him for?"—because I was a new man.

"Well," Burgess says, "he can sing."

Old Newman snorted and said: "If you think I'm going to pay forty dollars a month for a music box for you fellows all winter, you're crazy."

And Burgess said: "That's all right. The night never gets so dark nor the river so deep that Teddy isn't with the herd."

When we started out to camp on Sunday Creek that afternoon, I still had a bottle of whisky. There's an old range law that says: "No whisky with the wagon," but I brought this bottle along and set it down under a clump of sagebrush.

Burgess said: "Say, you know it's against the rule to bring whisky into camp."

I said: "Sweetheart, your camp ends a hundred feet from the fire."

That was true. A hundred feet from the fire is all you can claim; that takes in the wagon and the horse corral, and if you order a man out of camp, you can't order him no further than that. But within that line it's your property and if a stranger rides up you say: "Come into camp and sit down," just the way you do in a house. Lots of them wouldn't get off their horses until you asked them. I know I wouldn't.

Anyway Burgess laughed, and the bottle stayed out in the sagebrush, and we'd all go out and visit it until it was gone. It didn't last long. But that was the only time I ever knew of an exception to the rule about whisky with the wagon. Everybody knew that drinking and cattle didn't mix, and there was never any trouble.

The second herd was three or four days behind us, going up to the mouth of the Musselshell. We got through without any trouble, but when they reached the Big Dry, north of the Yellowstone, they struck a terrible snowstorm one night, and they all like to have froze. They built a row of fires, and the men who were off guard led their night horses back and forth in front of them all night, to keep them from dying of the cold—because the night horses were staked, and couldn't move around and keep warm like the horse herd. And the fires and the walking was all that kept the men from freezing as well, because they didn't have any warm blankets. Them henskins[1] they brought up from Texas wouldn't cast a shadow on the ground if you'd hang them up.

After the work was all done that fall, twenty men from the two herds went down to Miles City. And about fifteen out of the twenty—including all who were caught in that blizzard—got on the train and went back to Texas. Some of them was in such a hurry they didn't even stop in town for a drink, but went and sat in the station until the train pulled out. They'd got their bellyful of Montana.

[1] Thin blankets.

Miles City—Buffalo Hunters, Bullwhackers, and Cowboys—
The N Bar Outfit Trees the Marshal—
The Girls—Knight of the Plains—
Cowboy Annie

After we got up to the mouth of the Musselshell that fall, we had to build corrals and brand a lot of the cattle that didn't have anything on them except the road brand. But the corrals were small, and there wasn't room for two men to rope at a time, so instead of stretching them out between two ropes on horseback, the way you're supposed to do with full-grown cattle, we were on the ground tailing them down as if they were calves. I only weighed 135 pounds, but I was down in the corral wrestling those big steers and holding the ropes by hand to stretch them. They were big and strong and they kicked like the devil when the brand went on them. I got rope burns that injured those cords in the palms of my hands, so that when I got older they crippled up on me, and that is why today I can't open but the first two fingers of each hand.

You know if you get a name for doing something they will always put it on you. It's like these fellows that don't mind riding broncs. Once it gets known that they're willing to do it, if there's a mean horse in the outfit they'll get him in their string every time. I was good at wrestling calves even if I was small, so I'd always get the job. But I didn't like to ride broncs—said I was afraid of them. Well, I was.

Lots of them were the same way. No good cowhand would work on a horse that was going to go to bucking with him in the middle of the herd. A green horse was all right for a long ride. But not when you were working with cattle.

After we got all the fall work done, about Thanksgiving, we went to town with two wagons to load up with grub for the winter. Anyway, that was one reason for going. A lot of them went in with the wagons, especially the men that wasn't coming back. They took the road, but three of us took our horses and a pack outfit, and we cut across the country and saved two days.

Miles City was the cow town then for the north end of the range. The first Texas herds got up there in '80, and the Northern Pacific reached it in the fall of '81. There were plenty of places along the line where Montana and Wyoming cattle could have been shipped, but Miles City had the best stockyards and, besides that, it appealed to Wyoming cowmen because they could follow Tongue River in and have good grass and water all the way.

Before we got there it was an army post and buffalo hunters' town, and those people were still around there when we first come in with the herds. I suppose you would call it picturesque, though we never thought of it that way. It was the big city to us. In 1884 it had two blocks of business section, besides some scattered houses. The only other regular street besides Main Street was Park, that ran alongside a little grove of cottonwood trees. In the summertime men that didn't have fifty cents to sleep in a hotel would take their blankets and spread them in the little park, under the trees; not cowpunchers, but buffalo hunters and bullwhackers and that class of people. They was always going broke in town. There was a saloon man in Miles City named Charlie Brown. He had the Cottage Saloon and he kept a big bowl of Mulligan stew standing on the stove all the time, and he would say, "Just help yourself." If they wanted to, they could take their blankets and bed down on the floor, and in the morning he would give them a free drink. He figured that when they got a hundred dollars they would blow it right over his bar, and they did.

A cowpuncher would never hang around town after he run out of money. He would get on his horse and drift back out to the ranch. Oh, there was exceptions once in a great while, when a fellow got a mash on a girl. I know of one case where a cowpuncher went in town and gave his sweetheart a hundred dollars, which was all he had in the world, and she kept him all winter. She lived in kind of a little crib behind a saloon, a log shack with just a bedroom and kitchen. He moved in there, and when she had company he slept in the kitchen or in the saloon. But I guess that is what you would call an old story.

Cowpunchers and buffalo hunters didn't mix much, and never would have even if the buffalo hunters hadn't went out of the picture when they did. The buffalo hunters was a rough class—they had to be, to lead the life they led. That buffalo slaughter was a dirty business. They would have two skinners working with each pair of hunters, and the hunters would go out and round up a bunch of buffalo, and shoot down all they could. The skinners would follow after in a wagon and take the hides. But when it got dark they would quit, leaving maybe ten or twenty carcasses that would freeze up solid, and next spring they would just lie there on the prairie and rot, hides and all. Riding the range, you would find lots of skeletons with pieces of hide still sticking to them. It was all waste.

All this slaughter was a put-up job on the part of the government, to control the Indians by getting rid of their food supply. And in a way it couldn't be helped. But just the same it was a low-down dirty way of doing the business, and the cowpunchers as a rule had some sympathy with the Indians. You would hear them say it was a damn shame.

The buffalo hunters didn't wash, and looked like animals. They dressed in strong, heavy, warm clothes and never changed them. You would see three or four of them walk up to a bar, reach down inside their clothes and see who could catch the first louse for the drinks. They were lousy and proud of it.

The cowpunchers was a totally different class from these other fellows on the frontier. We was the salt of the earth, anyway in our own estimation, and we had the pride that went with it. That was why Miles City changed so much after the trail herds got there; even the women changed. Because buffalo hunters and that kind of people would sleep with women that cowpunchers wouldn't even look at, and it was on our account that they started bringing in girls from eastern cities, young girls and pretty ones. Those girls followed us up, like I told you, and we would meet old pals in new places.

But I missed out. There was one of those girls named Lily Davis, who was in Lincoln the winter and spring of '82, and I spent most of that winter staying in town with her. I really thought a lot of her—she was awfully kind and jolly and a good scout—didn't try to work you out of every damn cent you had. Next year she and her girl friend turned up in Cheyenne, and from there I heard they went to the Black Hills. They came to Miles City in '83, but Lily left before I got there and went to Butte. I never saw her again.

But I was starting to tell you about how the N Bar outfit went to Miles City in the autumn of '84, and treed the city marshal and run the **P. I.**s into the hills. That was a great cowpuncher saying in the old days. They would always come back from a trip to town bragging about how they had treed the marshal. One reason for the saying was that when those boys got ready to raise hell, the marshal would just disappear. Half the time he belonged to the saloon men. As for the P. I.s, the rest of the word is *m, p, s*. All them city marshals and tinhorn gamblers had a woman and lived off her, and running the P. I.s into the hills meant that after the boys had a few drinks they wanted to see the girls, and the P. I.s had to hide out. Cowboys sure had it in for P. I.s.

There was three of us from the N Bar that stayed in Miles City that week, John Burgess, John Bowen, and me. Burgess and Bowen were wagon bosses, and they were a little bit older than the rest of us with the outfit; I think Burgess was twenty-seven. But their dignity didn't bother them any when they were in town. I remember some fellow come around wanting Burgess for something and he asked Zeke Newman where he was. Newman said: "If you're looking for any of them N Bar tigers, you'll find them at the parlor house."

Mag Burns'[1] parlor house that was; on a side street, Number 44. I was at Maggie Burns' the time my singing got me in trouble and the marshal pretty nearly had me treed instead of the other way around. Three of us was in the parlor of Maggie Burns' house giving a song number called "The Texas Ranger." John Bowen was playing the piano and he couldn't play the piano, and Johnny Stringfellow was there sawing on a fiddle and he couldn't play a fiddle, and I was singing, and between the three of us we was raising the roof. And Maggie—the redheaded, fighting son of a

1 Ficitious name.

gun—got hopping mad and says: "If you leather-legged sons of bitches want to give a concert, why don't you hire a hall? You're ruinin' my piano."

So I got mad, too, and I says: "If I had little Billy here" —well, I told her what I'd do to her piano. And John Bowen said: "Go and get him, Teddy, go and get him." That was enough for me. I went across the street and got Billy out of the livery stable, and came back and rode him through the hall and into the parlor, where I dismounted. And as soon as I got in the parlor, Maggie slammed the door and locked it, and called the police.

But there was a big window in the room, that was low to the ground, and Billy and me got through it and got away. We headed for the ferry on a dead run, and that is the origin of the story that Charlie Russell tells in *Rawhide Rawlins,* about me telling that jack rabbit to "get out of the way, brother, and let a fellow run that can run." I got to the ferry just as it was pulling out, and jumped Billy across a little

piece of water onto the apron. The sheriff got there right after me and he was hollering at the ferryman to stop. And the ferryman hollered back at him: "This fellow has got a gun the size of a stovepipe stuck in my ribs, and I ain't agoing to stop."

It all blew over and I came back to Miles City the next day.

Cowboy Annie lived at Mag Burns' house. She was the N Bar outfit's girl. They were all stuck on her except the bookkeeper, the nigger cook, and me. Her pal was my sweetheart. But Cowboy Annie surely had the rest of them on her string, and that was true as long as the N Bar outfit in that part of the country held together. She used to tickle me to death. She had a little book, with all her fellows' names written down in it, and she would say to me: "Now just make all the brands in it, Teddy." The boys wouldn't all get to town at once as a rule, but when they did there was hell apopping.

Burgess was really gone on her. I introduced them that fall in Miles City, and it lasted until she got played out and went to Fort Assiniboine, on Milk River, to a soldier dive. She took to drinking and bad acting before that—rode her horse up and down the street and got arrested, and went on downhill from there. The soldiers was the bottom. They used to say out in this country that when a woman left the dogs she'd go to the soldiers. But all that was quite a few years later. She was at her height in Miles City, an awful pretty girl, with dark eyes and hair. And she could work Burgess for anything.

One day she said to him, kind of coaxing, "Oh, Johnny, I've got a sealskin coat and cap coming from Chicago, and there's still $150 against it at the express office. Won't you get it out for me?"

He made some excuse—said he didn't have $150. She pouted. "I don't care. Jim Green[2] will get it out for me." He was foreman of the S T outfit. And Johnny fell like a ton of bricks. He said: "I've got just as much money as any S T son of a gun in Montana." And he went down to the express office and got it for her.

I believe he'd have married her if she'd have had him. She could have had her pick of a dozen fellows, but she didn't want any of them. I guess after the life she'd led she couldn't see living on a homestead, getting up early in the morning, working hard, having a lot of kids. The girls like her that quit and settled down was usually worn out and half dead before they did it.

There was a lot of fellows in the eighties who were glad enough to marry them, but I never would have married that kind. I always secretly had in my heart the hopes of meeting a nice girl. I always wanted a cow ranch and a wife, and I got them both. And it was hard going at times, but believe me it was worth it.

I got to talking to one of those chippies out in this country about thirty years back, about the life, and the different places she had been, and so forth, Her name was Myrtle, and her and her sister came up here to Gilt Edge for payday. I was riding into town, and she had knocked the heel off her shoe and I got a nail and fixed it for her. Afterwards when she had more or less reformed and was running a decent rooming house in Lewistown, I stayed there one time and got to talking with her. I said: "Before I was married, I used to hop around among you folks a good deal and I don't see how you stand it. It looks like a hell of a life to me."

She said: "Well, you know there's a kind of a fascination about it. Most of the girls that are in it wouldn't leave it if they could."

2 Fictitious name.

Miles City

Some of those girls in Miles City were famous, like Cowboy Annie and Connie the Cowboy Queen. Connie had a $250 dress embroidered with all the different brands—they said there wasn't an outfit from the Yellowstone down to the Platte, and over in the Dakotas too, that couldn't find its brand on that dress.

We all had our favorites after we got acquainted. We'd go in town and marry a girl for a week, take her to breakfast and dinner and supper, be with her all the time. You couldn't do that in other places. There was two girls I knew in Lincoln—it was Lily Davis and her pal—that I wanted to take to a show one night. I had to take them in a hack, because if they had walked down the street they would have been arrested. But Lincoln had a very religious mayor and was getting civilized. You couldn't walk around with those girls in the daytime like you could in Miles City.

Things were different down South, too, from what they were up North. In Texas men couldn't be open and public about their feelings towards those women, the way we were. There was a fellow who fell in love with a madam in Miles City, and he was a prominent man. He used to take her everywhere. She had another lover at the same time, a deputy sheriff, and they came near having a fight over it. Everybody was looking for it. They was just dodging one another. But finally the second fellow died, and the first one married her and they went to Mexico.

I suppose those things would shock a lot of respectable people. But we wasn't respectable and we didn't pretend to be, which was the only way we was different from some others. I've heard a lot about the double standard, and seen a lot of it, too, and it don't make any sense for the man to get off so easy. If I'd have been a woman and done what I done, I'd have ended up in a sporting house.

I used to talk to those girls, and they would tell me a lot of stuff, about how they got started, and how in Chicago and those eastern cities they wasn't allowed on the streets, how their clothes would be taken away from them, only what they needed in the house, so it was like being in prison. They could do as they pleased out here. And they were human, too. They always had money and they would lend it to fellows that were broke. The wagon bosses would come around looking for men in the spring, and when a fellow was hired he would go to his girl and say: "I've got a job, but my bed's in soak." Or his saddle or his six-shooter or his horse. And she would lend him the money to get it back and he would pay her at the end of the month. Cowboy Annie was the kind who would always dig down and help the boys out, and so were a lot of them. They always got it back. I never knew of but one case where a fellow cheated one of those girls, and I'll bet he never tried it again. He come up the trail for one of the N Bar outfits—not ours, but the one on the Niobrara—and he went with Cowboy Annie for a week. Then he got on his horse and rode away, owing her seventy dollars. First he went back to the Niobrara, but the foreman of the outfit heard of it and fired him, then he went down in Texas, but they heard of it down there and fired him again. And the N Bar fellows took up a collection and paid her what he owed, because they wouldn't have a thing like that standing against the name of the outfit.

That shows you how we were about those things. As Mag Burns used to say, the cowpunchers treated them sporting women better than some men treat their wives.

Well, they were women. We didn't know any others. And any man that would abuse one of them was a son of a gun. I remember one time when a P. I. beat up on his girl for not coming through with enough money or something like that, and a fellow I knew jumped on him and half-killed him. The man hadn't done nothing to him. It was none of his business. It was just the idea of mistreating a woman.

I can tell you about something that happened to me one time, and the close shave I had, all because of these notions of chivalry toward women, no matter who they were. I was with a girl at a house one night—Omaha, I called her, because she said that was where she came from. This happened in Miles City, the winter I was with the F U F, and I was just twenty-three years old.

In the middle of the night we heard this fracas downstairs—a woman's screams and then something that sounded like a body falling. I thought, "Somebody's been killed, sure." And then I heard footsteps coming up the stairs. I got up and got my six-shooter and went and stood at the head of the stairs, and there was a woman coming up, slowly. She had on a white nightgown, and the front of it was all covered with blood. I found out later that it just came from a cut on her forehead. But it looked terrible. I heard someone coming behind her, and I called down: "If you take one more step, I'll shoot you." And I would have, because I thought I couldn't do less.

Well, the woman was Willie Johnson, who ran the house. She was about two years older than I was. She came into the room, and I helped her to get fixed up. She was in an awful mess, with blood all over her from that cut on her forehead, and a black eye that he gave her, this man who was her sweetheart.

"I don't care for the black eye, Teddy," she whimpered, "but he called me a whore."

Can you beat that? It was what she was. I was never so disgusted in my life. I was such a damn fool. I might have

killed that man and got into a peck of trouble. Knight of
the plains. Had to protect all females. Lord!

After I got older and got more sense I got onto some of
it, and I got so at least I wouldn't believe all the things they
told me about myself. After I had heard it all a hundred
times I got so I would just laugh when they flattered me up
and told me I was so wonderfully this, that, and the other.
And they would say, "What are you laughing at?" I never
told them.

But the black-eye story was another one of the things
that were repeated all around, and got to be a by-word with
the cowpunchers. So that when I was on herd, somebody
would yell across in a high-pitched voice: "Oh, Ted-dee! I
don't mind the black eye . . ." and so forth. But just the
same it shows the way I felt about those women at that time.

If you were good to them, they'd appreciate it, and believe me, they had ways of repaying a kindness, as I ought
to know. One time a few years after this I was shipping beef
at a station on the N. P., and I went to a honky-tonk, and
there was a girl there that I had knowed in Miles City. We
were drinking and fooling around, and after awhile I said:
"Come on, let's go back to your room." She said: "No,
Teddy. Not with you." A few minutes later I saw her going
back there with another fellow. Well, she had to live.

And before that in Lincoln there was a girl called Eddie,
that I took on after my pal Lily Davis left and went to
Cheyenne. She was a newcomer in the same house, and while
I don't know whether she was new to the game or not, she
had just landed in Lincoln and she didn't have any good
clothes. She told me about it, and told me she couldn't com-
pete with the other girls. I wasn't much more than a kid
then, but I had money, and I staked her to an outfit. She

paid it all back eventually. And in return she told me a lot of things that stood me in good stead.

I always had money because I didn't gamble—only a little, now and then. I couldn't see giving it to them tinhorns. You knew they were going to take it away from you. And besides, I never had time to gamble; I couldn't sit still long enough; I always had to be up, talking, singing, drinking at the bar. I was so happy and full of life, I used to feel, when I got a little whisky inside me, that I could jump twenty feet in the air. I'd like to go back and feel that way once more. If I could go back I wouldn't change any part of it.

A night or two before we left town that fall, we were all together with the girls, drinking and having a good time, and I got dressed up. Cowboy Annie put her gold chain around my neck, and wound her scarf around the crown of my Stetson, and this dressing up in a woman's clothes started us talking about the stunt that Jake Des Rosses pulled at Ogallala the year before. There was a dance going on and not enough women to go around, which was the usual way of it in that country, and a couple of fellows got left without a partner. So one of them said: "I'll fix that." And he went in a back room—this was in a honky-tonk, of course—and he came out with a pair of woman's white ruffled drawers pulled on over his pants. He and the other fellows danced around, and it brought down the house. We'd all heard the story. It went all over the range, and it even got into books.[3]

So we were talking about it and Cowboy Annie turned to me.

"Would you do that?" she says.

I said yes, naturally. So she pulled them off, and I put

[3] Edgar Beecher Bronson's *Reminiscences of a Ranchman.*

them on over my pants. And we all paraded down the street, me with my gold necklace and the trimming on my hat and Cowboy Annie's drawers on. The whole town turned out to see us. It turned the place upside down.

Well, that was the kind of wild, crazy stunt that gave me my reputation. They'd tell about a thing like that clear down to Texas, especially anything that came up that was funny. The reps would ride around to the roundups and carry it along, and in the winter time the grub line riders would carry it. We had to talk about something. It was all the fun we had.

Next day, or the day after that, we all left for the mouth of the Musselshell. In the morning when we was ready Burgess wasn't there. Somebody had seen his horse, with the reins dropped, standing in front of the parlor house, and I went up there to get him. He was in Cowboy Annie's room. He had been to the bank and got the money and gone back there to pay her, for the week. And when I came in—because I was a friend of them both—she flipped back the pillow cover and showed me the yellow pile nested there—seventy dollars in gold.

After that, going back to the mouth of the Musselshell, I made up a song about Cowboy Annie,[4] that went:

> *Cowboy Annie was her name,*
> *And the N Bar outfit was her game.*

and ended up:

> *And when the beef is four years old,*
> *We'll fill her pillow slips with gold.*

I still had Cowboy Annie's ruffled drawers that she gave

4 See page 228.

me that night, and I put them on a forked stick and carried them that way to the mouth of the Musselshell, like a flag. And before we left, my girl took one of her stockings off and tied it around my arm, you know, like the knights of old, and I wore *that* to the mouth of the Musselshell.

After we got up there, I had the flag hanging on the wall of the cabin, until Harry Rutter got sore one day and tore it down and throwed it in the stove. He said it wasn't decent. And no more it was.

13

The Mouth of the Musselshell—
An Awful Lot of Montana History—Jenny Is Scalped—
We Turn Them Loose on the Musselshell—
Bad Luck Still Holds

We spent that whole winter at the mouth of the Mussel-shell, which comes in where the Missouri River makes its big bend, 135 miles east of Great Falls. As I believe I said before, this was the third N Bar outfit. The 4,000 head of cattle that they trailed up here from Texas was all steers, and they was going to run it as a steer outfit, no cows or calves, just bringing in more steers from time to time and double-wintering them and shipping the beef. That was the plan, but it never worked out.

There was an old trading fort at the mouth of the Mus-selshell that was just standing there deserted, and we took it over that winter and lived in it. There were several log buildings and a stockade and corrals, and a two-room house that was quite a good size as log houses go, but there is nothing left of any of it any more. It all went into the river years ago.

The house was built for a storeroom and store at the old trading post, and it had a counter and a puncheon floor. This was the old store that was used by Billy Downs and the gang of horse thieves, and that he was living in when Gran-ville Stuart and his raiders came and got him and hanged him in the summer of '84, a few months before we got up there. They hanged or shot fourteen of them at different places along the Missouri River, including this Billy Downs, who was more or less the bookkeeper and storekeeper for the bunch. Before he met his end, in the early part of July, the vigilantes come for him another time. They say it was to warn him, but I don't know. Anyway they didn't get him the first time, because he knew they were coming. And he dug a hole under the heavy timbers of that puncheon floor, just big enough for himself and a jug of water and some food, and he hid under there until they went away. I know that is true, because when we took down the counter to make room for our bunks, we found some loose timbers underneath. And we lifted them up, and there was his hole that he hid in. It looked like a little grave.

That flat at the mouth of the Musselshell has seen an awful lot of Montana history, and bloody history at that, but soon it will all be under the water of Fort Peck dam. There had been two forts on the site before we got up there fifty-four years ago, and the one we took over was the second. You see that location always appealed to people in the early days as a good place to start a town. The bluffs widen out there, leaving this big flat where the Musselshell River winds along into the Missouri, and a couple of creeks come into the Musselshell, and there is lots of room for houses. The first fort was built in 1868 by some Helena business-men, who were promoting a town at the mouth of the Mus-selshell to take the river trade away from Fort Benton. The idea looked good, but there was a couple of things the matter with it, and the worst one was Indians.

The place was always a bone of contention with the In-dians, especially the Sioux. They didn't seem to want any-body to settle there, I don't know why, unless it was because they always used that place for crossing back and forth over the river with their hunting parties. Old-timers have told me that when there wasn't any trouble anywhere else in Montana there would still be raiding at Fort Musselshell. Henry MacDonald said that at the mouth of the Musselshell and in the country right around it there was more than thirty different massacres of white people by Indians.

I got a lot of this early history from MacDonald, who was a trapper at the fort when they had all the trouble. He was a little chap, not over five feet, five inches tall, and he was a Pony Express rider and a great hunter and Indian fighter. What I didn't get from him I got from Pike Landusky and two or three other fellows who was there at the time. They told me that during the spring of '69 there was always somebody waiting in the hills to snipe them, and they was afraid to go out from the post only in bunches. That was the spring Jenny Smith got scalped, that woman I told you about who was living in Forsyth in '83. Some men were getting out timber up the Musselshell, and Jenny and another of them women, a squaw, I think, was taking their dinner out to them, when a bunch of Indians jumped them. The second woman was killed, and Jenny was wounded and scalped alive. She played dead while they were taking her scalp, and that was the only thing that saved her. I don't know how she did it, but she did.

A few weeks after that was when they had the big fight at the mouth of the Musselshell and killed thirteen Indians, and that put an end to the raiding for a little while. They had been sniping at the settlement all the time, like I told you, but they played the coward and would run off if anybody opposed them. Pretty soon it got so all the white men got brave enough to run out and chase them when they came around. One day a little bunch of Indians had come in and started some trouble, and the whites was chasing them up the flat as usual, when a shot from one side killed the front man. They found out they was just about to run into an ambush. It turned out there was sixty or seventy Indians down in a cul-de-sac, I suppose you'd call it, a sort of a pocket the water had washed out along the Mussel-shell, or it might have been one of those old cut banks where the river had changed its course.

Henry MacDonald and a couple of other men swum the river and got around behind them in those thick willows on the riverside, and they opened up on them from there. Meanwhile the rest of the people had come out from the settlement and had got out in front of them, on the bank. And it started to rain, and that wet the Indians' powder and put their old-fashioned guns out of commission. Mac said it was an awful sight to see their terror when they found out they were trapped. Their eyes was just popping, and they ran every which way, like rats. He said you could hear them panting in that quiet, and some of them ran right into the guns.

Thirteen were killed in the cul-de-sac, and thirty more of them died on the way to camp. Jenny was watching the fight from a bastion of the fort, and they say that when the boys came in with thirteen fresh scalps she felt consoled for having to wear a wig.

Little Mac, as they called him, was wearing a whole buck-skin suit when he swum the river, and the trousers length-ened so much when they got wet that they tripped him up. So he took them off and went through the fight naked from below the waist. After it was over he was on his way back to the settlement to get some clothes, when he ran onto a couple of Crow Indian squaws that were living at the post with the white men. He said their attentions was quite em-barrassing to him.

It was after that fight that Liver-eating Johnson held up a piece of an Indian's liver, that he had cut out, and said: "We'll have liver for breakfast." I've been told by fellows who was there that he never did eat that liver, but he always went by the name after that. Those Indians had been picking on the settlement for a long time and there wasn't any mercy shown. Old Cap' Andrews, the trader at the fort, cut off ten of the Indians' heads and boiled them and scraped the flesh off, and put them up on stakes on the stockade. They say the sight was quite a shock to the lady passengers on the first steamboat of the season, when she got up there on the spring rise a couple of days later.

After the Indian troubles that spring, the company that operated the main post give up and went out of business and most of the settlement went with it. The first fort and the houses was all in the river by the time we got there, except that you could still see the trench where they sank the logs for the stockade.

But there was another trader at the mouth of the Musselshell, Colonel George Clendennin, and after the first company quit, he rebuilt and refortified his own post, and stuck it out four more years. He moved up the river to Carroll in '74, and his old fort was the one we lived in. From the time he left until we came in there ten years later, there was nobody much at the mouth of the Musselshell, except a few woodhawks and those outlaws.

Since that time I have read quite a few historical writings about the mouth of the Musselshell, and I notice that the writers, knowing all about how many people was murdered and scalped and hanged there in the early days, always talk about what a gloomy-looking place it was. But we were new-come there, we hadn't heard those stories, and it looked all right to us. As far as scenery goes, I don't see anything wrong with it today, only it is lonely and desolate. You can go there and back from Lewistown in a day by car, in good weather, but it is way the hell and gone over steep hills and a narrow gumbo road. If it rained, you'd be stuck there for a week. There is nothing in there at all except a few ranches, and most of them are deserted on account of the dam coming. Up to a few years ago they used to run one of them old cable ferries across the river, but it is stove up now and pulled out on the bank. Everything is changed from the way it used to be, only the old Big Muddy rolls along, chewing at her banks like she always has. And even that is going to be changed, because all that part of the river will be flooded by the dam.

It is very rough country in there.[1] Granville Stuart used to say it was so rough that the magpies' wings got broke flying over it. Going back from the river there are great big timbered breaks that look like the foothills of a range of mountains; and back of that, all those coulees head out on a big level divide, covered with grass and scattered bull pines. You can drive for miles along the top of the divide without seeing a fence, and the country looks just the way it did a thousand years ago.

After we got up to the mouth of the Musselshell with that herd, we turned the drags loose first, at a little creek that didn't have any name. So we called it Drag Creek. And Drag Creek it is today, as you can see by the sign on the bridge where the road crosses it.

We turned the string loose when we got down on the flat, and the leads we started up Crooked Creek, which is the

[1] Understatement. It is magnificent. The only way to give a picture of it is to talk in terms of the Grand Canyon, which vastly exaggerates a pattern repeated countless times along the rivers of the west. It is this pattern which you think of when you see the colored escarpments along the Missouri.

last stream that comes into the Musselshell before you get to the mouth. The cattle was supposed to graze away from the river, up on to the divide, but we couldn't keep them there because those timbered breaks was full of bear. It may be that the old bad luck that lived at the mouth of the Musselshell still held against us, or rather against the N Bar outfit. Because the next year they give it up, and quit that place, and moved all their cattle down onto the Big Dry.

14

Rocky Point—Recipe for Indian Whisky—
Winter in a Cow Camp—
I Pick a Wife—Fired Again—
I Go to Work for the D H S

After we got back to the mouth of the Musselshell from Miles City, we all settled down for the winter. There was nothing else to do. Our outfit was the only one in that country, we had no neighbors of any kind, and the nearest town, if you could call it a town, was Rocky Point, forty-five miles up the river by horseback. There was a few stores at Rocky Point, and a saloon run by a man named Marsh, and three white women. One was Mrs. Marsh, a very nice lady who kept the eating house. She had a daughter. And there was also a woman they called Big Ox, who was one of those haybags that used to follow the buffalo camps.

They had the damnedest names, those big old fat buffalo women. Most of them can't even be told. Our girls, that followed us up from the South, never had names like that. They were called Cowboy Annie and Gentle Annie and the Texas Steer and such—the worst name I ever heard among them was Tough Lil.

But they was a different kind of people. There was nothing like that up here. We was in a wilderness and we had to make the best of it. As for Big Ox, I have heard men say that when a man was starving he would eat crumbs and worse than crumbs.

There was a few other towns along the Missouri River, but they was further away from us than Rocky Point and no different when you got there. Claggett and Carroll were between Rocky Point and Fort Benton. There was ferries at both of them, and after the Great Northern was built, the freight teams would cross over there, taking supplies to Fort Maginnis. But all those river towns except Fort Benton have practically disappeared today. There isn't any reason for them any more, now that the steamboats, and the buffalo, and the bull teams, and the army posts, and the Indians, too, are all a thing of the past.

About eighteen years ago there was another spell of activity along the river, but it was a different kind. In 1919 and 1920 every foot of that country back from the Missouri on the south side was taken up for dry farms, which was a crime, because that is grazing country, not farming country, and all those bohunk farmers did was to carve up good range for nothing but starvation in the end. There is not a sign of them today. They've all gone; even the empty houses have

gone; you can drive along there for miles and not see a thing except once in a long way an old claim shack, that hasn't been tore down yet for the lumber in it, and a few fence posts with the wires stripped off them. But the hills are still there. And this summer, 1938, the grass came back the way it used to be and waved in the wind. And oh, boy, but it was a beautiful sight.

The winter of '84–'85 John Bowen stayed at Rocky Point, to ride that end of the range and watch for rustlers. He took his own bed and slept in Ritchie and Collins' warehouse, and the outfit paid his board with Mrs. Marsh. In the warehouse Ritchie and Collins had a barrel of Indian whisky setting on a block and a tin cup on top of it, and you could go in there and help yourself. That was how cheap it was.

Now I'll give you the recipe for Indian whisky, that was invented by the Missouri River traders in the early days. You take one barrel of Missouri River water and two gallons of alcohol. Then you add two ounces of strychnine to

make them crazy—because strychnine is the greatest stimu-
lant in the world—and three plugs of tobacco to make them
sick—because an Indian wouldn't figure it was whisky unless it made him sick—and five bars of soap to give it a bead,
and half a pound of red pepper, and then you put in some
sagebrush and boil it until it's brown. Strain this into a
barrel and you've got your Indian whisky, that one bottle
calls for one buffalo robe, and when the Indian got drunk
it was two robes. And that's how some of the traders made
their fortune.

I never heard of it being sold anywhere except in those
posts along the Missouri. White men didn't drink much
of it because it wasn't fit stuff for a white man. Only they
did drink it sometimes.

To show you what Indian whisky was, I can tell you a
story about the time Harry Rutter came down to Rocky
Point that winter on a visit. We'd left him out at the mouth
of the Musselshell in charge of the outfit the time we all
went to Miles City, and this was the first he'd been in a town
since the day we was camped on Sunday Creek and him and
me went into Miles City on a sneak. He was celebrating
around for awhile, and he got pretty full in the saloon.
When it got late, he came back with John Bowen to the warehouse and put his bed down, and the two of them laid there
and talked. And as they talked, Harry kept helping himself
out of this barrel of Indian whisky. Finally he stretched out
and got ready to go to sleep, and then he said to John, very
solemn and careful: "John, will you do me a favor? Will
you close my eyes for me?" He was so drunk he couldn't close
his eyes.

Well, that was Indian whisky for you. We laughed about
it all winter and told the story around. A little thing like that
was a big kick to us, you understand, a bunch of men out

there by ourselves, with no newspapers or anything else to read, and nothing to do but get up and feed the stove.

The outfit was keeping us for the winter, as the custom was in those days, because good hands were scarce and it paid the owners to keep the men who knew their range and brands, so they would have a crew together when spring came. But we were laid off for two or three months without pay, there being no work of any kind. They didn't feed hay to the cattle in the early days of the open range; and in fact you couldn't have fed them even if you'd had the hay, because they scattered out so.

They tell a story about a fellow down in Texas who was stuck out in a horse camp by himself all winter, and when they went and hunted him up in the spring, they found he had his hat and coat draped on a stump and was shooting at it. He said: "I'm going to get the son of a bitch before he gets me."

We weren't as bad off as that at the mouth of the Musselshell, because we had company. But there wasn't anything to do except talk, and the talk soon ran out. We told each other everything we knew in a week. I knew about ten songs, and I sung them until everybody was sick of them. After that nobody had much to say. It's not that men get to fighting when they are holed up together, unless there is some reason for it, but they get kind of surly and quit talking. For awhile we'd go out and kill deer for meat, and that was something to pass the time. Over in those hills there were so many tracks, you'd think it was sheep. It was deer, hundreds of them. We ate them until we couldn't look at a piece of deer meat any more, and our beef was so tough, having walked all the way from South Texas, that you couldn't eat it either. So after that it was nothing but sowbelly and beans, three times a day.

We did have a couple of visitors. The summer before we came to the country, as I told you, the cowmen along the Musselshell had got together a party of vigilantes and hanged a lot of horse thieves. A few of the thieves got away across the Missouri, and one of the ones that escaped come back and stayed with us a week that winter. We didn't know his name. He just said he was out of grub. But another fellow that was staying with us told us afterwards who he was.

This other fellow, whose name was Frank Hansen, was camped with the horse thieves down the river when Granville Stuart killed a lot of them, and he came mighty near being hanged himself. We knew all about him, but we had to take him in just the same. The law of hospitality on the range was very strict. You had to feed and shelter your worst enemy if he came to your house in a storm, and if you refused him shelter, you had better leave that country.

This Hansen didn't get hanged because he didn't run away when the vigilantes came after him, though he had a good horse and might have made it. And besides that, one of the vigilantes knew him and vouched for him, so they let him go.

While he was with us, Hansen got to passing remarks about this fellow who had saved him, calling him a killer and cussing him out generally. It was true enough, I guess; the fellow had an ugly reputation, but as Harry Rutter said: "If a man had saved my life, I'd be more of a man than to cuss him." We didn't like Hansen after that, and there was some bickering, and we finally gave him some grub and turned him out of camp.

Visiting from one outfit to another, or riding the grub line as it was called, was one way a man could live during the winter. Lots of cowboys that could have stayed at home and lived off their own outfits would go visiting just for the sake of variety, and if they didn't have a horse, the company would give them one, and they would bring it back in the spring. Grub line riders were welcome wherever they stopped, because people who had been shut up all winter were glad to see new faces. They brought the news of the range.

It was a grub line rider who came down and told us about the pretty girls at the D H S. This was Granville Stuart's outfit, and it was located a long way to the south of us, in the Musselshell country, east of the Judith Mountains. The fellow told us that Granville Stuart had two grown daughters living at the ranch with him, and an old partner of his named Reece Anderson had three more. This was the biggest kind of news to lone cowpunchers. Most of us hadn't spoke to a nice girl in years. I know I hadn't; only to a few married ladies.

We talked them all over for days, and each of us picked out the one he was going to marry. It was something to talk about. And I remember I picked the younger one of Granville Stuart's two daughters, and I can tell you the reason. The grub line rider told us that Granville Stuart said he would give five hundred head of cattle to whoever married the oldest girl, though he said the little one, only fifteen years old, was the best-looking of the lot.

And I remember the horse wrangler said: "I'm going to take the oldest one and get the cattle." And I said: "I'll take the pretty little one." And we picked up our hats and went outside—said we were going right over to the D H S to get these girls, seventy-five miles away. We were joking, of course. We went about ten feet in the snow and come back —concluded we'd wait until spring.

But I did marry the little one, not quite five year later.

And that was about all there was to that winter. Except

that along toward spring Burgess decided to run a fence in the angle between the rivers and have a hay meadow there, so he put me to work digging post holes with a grub hoe. I wasn't strong on digging, especially not with a hoe. The ground was hard anyway. So I just scratched them, and when Burgess came to put up the posts that spring, he couldn't find the holes and he fired me.

After that I went to work for the D H S.

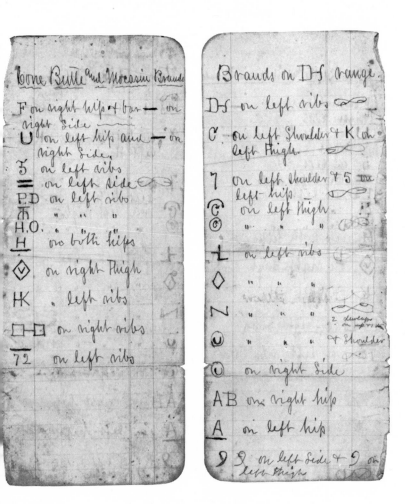

*Partial list of brands, in Granville Stuart's handwriting,
used by Teddy Blue in 1886*

Teddy Blue at the time of his marriage

15

Granville Stuart—
The Horse-thief Clean-up—
A Wonderful Outfit—Texas Greenhorns—
"You Take Them Out of the Saddle"

Everything that grub line rider had told us about the D H S sounded good to me, and I found out he hadn't exaggerated. It was a wonderful outfit, very well run, and the best I ever knew for a cowboy to work for. Granville Stuart fed well, never asked his men to work too hard, took a great interest in their welfare, and was always willing to help them when they were in trouble.

But he did more than that for them. Of all the big stockmen I ever knew or heard about, he was the fairest and the best friend to the cowpunchers. A great many of the big men in the cattle business were opposed to letting the cowboys own cattle, because they thought that if a man was allowed to have his own little bunch, with his own brand on them, it would encourage him in branding mavericks and other forms of stealing.

Granville Stuart never agreed with this. In '85 or '86, at the stock association meeting at Miles City, he made quite a speech, in which he tried very hard to get all the members to allow their cowpunchers to own cattle on the range. He said that 99 per cent of them were honest men, that if they were allowed to buy mavericks and own cattle it would give them a chance to get ahead and give them an interest in the range, that this would do more than anything else to stop rustling, since the boys were on the range all the time. He was voted down at the time, but he was right. The few outfits that did allow their men to own cattle never had any cause for complaint. Mr. Stuart himself stuck to his policy, against the opposition of some of his own partners.

I am trying to speak of him, not as a son-in-law, but just as a cowpuncher who worked on the range. Granville Stuart was the history of Montana. He made the first discovery of gold in Montana Territory, on Gold Creek in '57. That was what started the Virginia City stampede and all the rest of the gold excitement, and settled the Rocky Mountain region twenty years ahead of the plains.

He was a pioneer cattleman after that. Early in the spring of 1880, with all Montana to pick from, he took an old-time sheriff of Custer County as guide, and they went out to find good range for cattle. They swung around a big semicircle from west to east, crossed the Big and Little Horn rivers, the Yellowstone and the Musselshell, and kept going till they struck Ford's Creek, where he located the old D H S ranch. It was named after three partners, A. J. Davis of Butte, S. T. Hauser of Helena, and Granville Stuart. They made the brand this way, D–S, but they called it the D H S.

That fall they drove in 5,000 cattle from Oregon. During the winter Mr. Stuart and his personal partner, Reece Anderson, built log houses for the two families, with bunkhouses and stables and all the other buildings. They started to make the place a regular fort, with bastions on two corners, but as the government built a post at Fort Maginnis a few months later and the soldiers came in, this part was never finished. However, all the buildings had portholes, and the bunkhouse and stable were built about sixty feet apart, with a stockade in between to make a corral for the horses.

That first winter about twelve hundred Blackfeet were camped just above them and tried to run their horses off nearly every night. Although buffalo were plenty, they killed a lot of beef as well. The Blackfeet at this time were supposed to be settled and pacified; they had the whole country north of the Missouri River for a reservation, but they were always off it, hunting buffalo and raiding wherever they could. The government wouldn't have done anything if you'd asked them—not inside the next ten years—and I don't believe Mr. Stuart did ask them. On the frontier, men looked out for themselves.

So in the spring of '81 he took a bunch of men and simply told the Indians: "You pack up your tepees and rattle hocks out of here. And stay across the Missouri River after this or I will wipe you out." And he made it stick. Believe me, he had plenty of nerve.

The first time I ever saw him was at Miles City in April, '84. He was talking to Theodore Roosevelt, who at that time was a young man ranching near Medora, South Dakota. At that meeting in Miles City the Montana Stock Growers Association was formed, and plans were made to rid the range of the horse and cattle thieves. There was some discussion at the public meeting, and Teddy Roosevelt and the Marquis de Mores, who was also ranching in South Dakota, both came out strong for a war on the rustlers.[1] The stockmen voted against the proposition, publicly, because they did not want the rustlers to be warned in advance.

But after the regular meeting was over, they met again in executive session, and a vigilante organization was set up. It was arranged that Granville Stuart was to take charge

[1] Herman Hagedorn, in his *Roosevelt in the Bad Lands* (pp. 146–47) says that young Roosevelt and the Marquis de Mores were eager to accompany Granville Stuart on his expedition. But their services were refused by Mr. Stuart, who did not want any amateur frontiersmen along.

of the Maginnis part of the country, while other men took charge of the Little Missouri section and the Tongue River section. Executive committees, as they called them, were to do the hanging and shooting. It was all worked out to a *t,* on paper. But Granville Stuart was the one who followed it through.

It was Granville Stuart who organized and led the vigilantes and carried out the horse-thief clean-up at the mouth of the Musselshell in July of 1884. Some day I will tell the whole story of that clean-up, but it will take a long time. There was dozens of cases of so-called frontier justice in the history of the West, but I never knew of another one that gave less grounds to criticize it, when the facts were known. The rustlers of that day were a different class of men from the sneak thieves of today. They went in armed bands, took what they wanted by force, and defied arrest. It come to a showdown, fight or quit, and it was here that Granville Stuart showed the stuff he was made of. While lots of men went out of the territory for a trip and others sat in an office and said, "Go," Granville Stuart took his Winchester 50–95 express in his hand and led the way, and he never asked a man to go ahead of him. That gained him the respect of all the cowpunchers.

On July 3, 1884, a horse thief by the name of Sam McKenzie was hanged between Fort Maginnis and the D H S ranch. The next day fourteen men under Stuart left the D H S and rode to the mouth of the Musselshell. They hanged Billy Downs and another fellow there and two more at Rocky Point. The came back to the ranch, and two days later they left again for the woodyard at Bates Point, fifteen miles below the mouth of the Musselshell.

There used to be quite a few of those woodyards along the Missouri when the steamboats were running, and the people that wasn't wolfing or trapping or hunting buffalo or selling whisky to the Indians would make a living chopping wood for the boats to burn. But the boats quit in '83, when the Northern Pacific Railroad went through, and the buffalo were finished the same year. That left a lot of more or less honest men with no visible means of support, as the saying is. And those old deserted woodyards, with nothing there but a few shacks and a lot of big cottonwood stumps, made a wonderful hide-out for outlaws. The rough country along the Missouri was good for outlaws, too, and men who were tracking stolen horses would stop when they came to those breaks. They knew it wasn't any use to follow them in any further.

When Granville Stuart and his men got to Bates Point, they found twelve outlaws and had a fight. Five of the outlaws were killed and seven escaped. All but two of the ones that got away were captured later by soldiers at the Poplar Creek agency in eastern Montana, and turned over to a posse that was going to take them back to Fort Maginnis. While with the posse they met their death by hanging.

And that too happened at the mouth of the Musselshell. Just where you come down onto the flat, at the first crossing of the Musselshell about half a mile from the Missouri River, there is a grove of big cottonwood trees, and there is where they hanged them. Afterwards they cut them down and buried them in shallow graves. Or so I always understood, though of course I don't know for certain.

But I do know that when we got up there with that N Bar herd in the autumn of '84, just before we got to the first crossing of the Musselshell the cattle smelled something, and we had a little run. It was just the leads that ran and we stopped them without any trouble. But we never knew what it was they smelled until that fellow, Frank Hansen, that had been with the horse thieves, came and stayed with us that winter, and he told us about the corpses.

I didn't go to work for Granville Stuart until nearly a year after the clean-up. But quite a few of the cowboys knew about the big plans, in the spring of '84, and I was one of them. I couldn't help knowing, because I was working at that time for T. J. Bryan, the president of the Montana Stock Association, and I had a kind of a job with the vigilantes. I used to tell the rest of them that I was working for the Montana Assassination. They knew what I meant.

I was what was called a telegraph man. Our job was to carry messages back and forth, about the movements of certain men who were under suspicion. The password was the number twenty-six. "I've been waiting for you twenty-six hours." "I haven't seen you for twenty-six years." I had just one connection with the killing up in Montana, and that was hardly what you could call a connection. Two men called Rattlesnake Jake and Long-haired Owens, who were riding around the country together, were known to be thieves, and the Wyoming Stock Growers Association had a reward posted for one of them. About the first of July, 1884, I was working on the roundup close to Powder River, and I sent a telegram to Granville Stuart from Buffalo, Wyoming, letting him know that these men were on their way up into his territory. But before the executive committee up there could act, the two fellows run amuck at the Fourth of July celebration in Lewiston, and started a shooting fracas, and both got killed. I think they knew that they were doomed.

There was a lot of bitterness in the country against Granville Stuart after the raids. But he never denied anything, nor did he tell who was with him. Once I heard a woman accuse him of hanging thirty innocent men. He raised his hat to her and said: "Yes, madam, and by God, I done it alone."

Friends of the rustlers who were hanged even circulated stories that he had killed poor settlers in order to clear them off the range and have more room for his cattle. But every one who knew him knew that he was the friend of the settlers. For instance, in that awful winter of '86–'87, a settler by the name of Rehder had a nice bunch of milk cows and was making a living selling butter and eggs at Fort Maginnis. He came up to Stuart's ranch and told Mr. Stuart that his cattle were dying, that he had money but no hay, and his cattle was all he had to make a living for his family. And while Stuart's cattle were dying by thousands, Mr. Rehder got enough hay to save his cows. Rehder told me this himself.

Stuart gave settlers cows to milk and horses to work, branded their calves at roundup prices, and any honest man could get money from him. Honesty was his great hobby. And he was always interested in men who showed a desire to better themselves.

I can remember in the spring of '86, when I had saved

a little money, he persuaded me to send fifty dollars every two months to the bank in Helena. He always had a school teacher for the children at the ranch, and the other children of the neighborhood were invited to attend school there. In '81, the year after his arrival in the country, he built a schoolhouse and presented it to the district.

I am telling all this about him in order to show what kind of man it was who was accused of hanging innocent men. Granville Stuart lived on the frontier and he did what the frontier required of him. But he was a citizen for any state to be proud of.

When I came to the ranch, there were five boys and three girls, Katie, Mary, and Lizzie. Their mother, Granville Stuart's first wife, was a Shoshone Indian woman. He married her in 1862 when he was hunting gold. Lots of white men who took Indian wives put them aside after civilization come to the country, and married white women. But Granville Stuart always treated his Indian wife well, and was loyal to her until the day she died.

The spring of 1885 I didn't ride around the country, repping, the way I did the year before. I worked right here for the D H S, on the Maginnis roundup. Burgess was on hand with the N Bar wagon, and he came over to our camp one day at dinnertime, and tried to get me to go back to work for him after the roundup was over. I pointed to the mess box and said: "Sweetheart, they can't fire me from this outfit." I'd never seen such wonderful grub as they had at the D H S. They had canned tomatoes all the time, canned peaches even, while dried apples and prunes were the best you ever got in most cow outfits, and you were lucky to get those.

In Texas you wouldn't have got them. Those Texas outfits sure hated to give up on the grub. We had a Texas fellow repping with us on that roundup, eating with our wagon. The first day he was there we had hot cakes for breakfast, bread for dinner, and hot biscuits for supper. And when he saw the cook handing out the plate of biscuits, his eyes opened and he said: "Jesus Christ! Do you fellows have white bread three times a day?"

We used to have a lot of fun telling stories on them rawhides.[2] But we had been up here a year; we was old-timers in Montana by that time. In '83 and '84 and '85 a lot of Texas fellows was getting north to Montana for the first time, and for some of them it was the first they ever knew there was a world outside of Texas. They knew cows and horses backwards and forwards, but when it come to anything else they were from the sticks and no mistake. There was another story we used to tell about a Texas fellow who rode into a roundup camp at dinnertime, and they passed him the sugar, and he said: "No, thanks. I don't take salt in my coffee." He had never seen sugar before; only sorghum syrup.

That story could have been true. In the Texas outfits all they'd ever give them was cornbread and sowbelly and beans, except when they killed a beef. That was the reason so many of the Southern cowpunchers stayed in the North

[2] Derisive Northern name for Texas cowhands. It referred to the Texans' habit of mending whatever broke down or fell apart on the trail, from a bridle to a wagon tongue, by tying it up with strips of rawhide. To the Texans, on the other hand, the Northern cowpunchers were sagebrush men, or God-damn knock-kneed Oregonians.

Different methods of roping were one source of argument. The Oregon style of dally welting seems to have prevailed on the Northern range. But Southern opinion of it was summed up in the disgusted remark of Rafael, the Mexican already quoted by Teddy Blue. "Montana territory cowboys no too much account. T'row a big loop, all-a-time dally welt, cut off a t'umb, no tie like-a Tex." The charge about cutting off thumbs when the rope is not made fast is all too true. Montana and Wyoming are still full of cowboys with thumbs and fingers missing.

in spite of almost freezing to death; it was on account of the grub being so much better. The English outfits were the first ones responsible for that, and the rich Easterners. They had plenty of money and they wanted to be comfortable, and as they had to eat the same grub the men did, they'd have white flour and canned fruits, and all such luxuries. They began using tents, too, on the roundups, and some even had stoves in them.

On the roundup in '85 we were using a Sibley tent, the same as they had in the army. It was a circular tent, with the stove in the middle, and the men slept with their feet to the stove. The D H S was the first outfit in that part of the country to have one. Halfway through the roundup Burgess quit us to go and work another part of the range, and when he pulled out his wagon at Fort Maginnis, he asked if he could leave a rep with our wagon. We said: "All right, but there's no room in the tent." Burgess acted kind of superior about it. "My men ain't accustomed to tents," he said. "No real man would sleep in a tent."

And the very next night after leaving us, he and his men got down in the badlands on Crooked Creek, and a June storm came up—thunder and lightning and a downpour of rain. So they got in under a cut bank on Crooked Creek, and they took a tarp and fastened it to some bushes at the top of the bank, and staked it at the bottom, and they all crawled in there. And the creek raised four feet in the night and washed them out.

After he got out of the mud, Burgess went to Miles City and bought two tents. But he was stubborn and he would never admit he'd been wrong.

There was lots of them like that. They didn't know a thing in the world except cow, but they wouldn't give in to anybody. When I was with the N Bar there was a fellow working for their Powder River outfit by the name of John Green. He was from Texas like the rest of them, but he had been everywhere and seen everything, to hear him tell it. One morning at the ranch house they brought in the mail and the boss's wife was going after it.

"Oh, good," she says. "The catalogues have come. Now I can see what the Paris fashions are."

Old John wasn't going to let anybody get ahead of him, so he spoke up. "I been to Paris."

The lady says: "Hmph! How'd you ever get to Paris?"

"I went there with a beef herd."

"That's a likely story. How'd you get across the Atlantic Ocean with a beef herd?"

"Didn't cross no Atlantic Ocean. I went around the divide."

Those old-time Texas fellows may have been green, but at that they weren't much different from cowmen everywhere. In 1907, which wasn't so long ago as I look at it, I took a trip to Chicago with a trainload of beef, and there were a couple of other fellows along—one of them was named Sam Lawrence,[3] and he come from somewhere south of the Red River originally, though he hadn't seen Texas in years. After we got to Chicago we went out to see the sights, and first we had some drinks, and then we took a walk around, and we passed a sign that said: "Madam Somebody's Waxworks. For Men Only." Sam said: "Let's go in." The rest of us were agreeable, so we went on inside. There was a man standing at the door and he handed me a box of snuff—I said: "No, thank you," and walked on, before I noticed that he was part of the show. Pretty soon we came to a sort of show window, and inside it was a woman leaning away over, with one foot stuck straight up in the air

[3] This is just any old name. I've forgotten the one that Mr. Abbott used.

and a globe spinning around on it, and the other foot stuck out behind her. And all she had on was a little black velvet G string.

I was standing right next to her and I could hear her tick. But Sam was further away, and his vision was blurred anyhow, and he thought it was real. He said: "Poor little girl! The idea of a man making a woman do a thing like that before all these men! Why, hanging's too good for him." And he went on like that, working himself up.

I said: "Hold on, Sam. You're wrong. This is a waxworks layout. She's wound up." And I laid my hand on the leg that was stuck out behind her, to convince him.

He said: "The trouble with you you've lived with these no'thern-raised sons of bitches so long you don't respect a woman yourself."

Well, you take them out of the saddle and that's what they are.

16

Granville Stuart's Daughters—
The White Shirt Brigade—I Meet Charlie Russell—
"They've Been Living in Heaven for a Thousand Years"—
A Cheyenne Girl

It has taken me a long time to get back to the pretty girls at the D H S. The Stuart girls were half-breeds, but they were pretty, well-dressed, good dancers and very much sought after. By that time civilization was coming into the range, and there was parties several times a year at Lewistown and Fort Maginnis. In the spring you'd say to one of those girls: "What's the show to take you to the dance Fourth of July?" "Oh, I'm engaged for that." "Well, what's the show for the Thanksgiving dance?" "I'm engaged for that, too." If you wanted to get her, you'd have to ask her eight months ahead.

I had to laugh when I thought about that story of Mr. Stuart offering five hundred head of cattle to whoever married Katie, the oldest. He never did it. By the time I got over there he had to have a gun to keep them away. This wasn't so true of Mary because she was too young, and the third girl was just a kid. But Katie and the oldest Anderson girl could each have married a dozen men.

Those girls had every advantage there was to be given in that place and time. Mr. Stuart always had a schoolteacher living at the ranch. His second wife, who survives him, held that position for years. Whenever he went to Helena he

would bring back presents for them—a length of velvet for
a dress, or jewelry, or a peacock-feather fan. There was a
good deal of jealousy on account of it. The Stuart girls had
prettier and more expensive clothes than any of the others
in that country and was always dressed in the latest style,
and it drove the white girls wild.

The Stuarts and the Andersons all lived there really as
one family, though they had separate houses. I have heard
Eastern people talk about the loneliness of ranch life. It
makes me laugh when I think of the D H S. With all those
boys and girls growing up there, and the cowboys coming
and going even in winter, it was as lively a place as you'd
want to live. There was always a lot going on. I remember
one time when Mr. Stuart took the girls to Helena on a
visit and they caught the roller skating craze. When they
came back, they brought some skates with them, and they
fixed up a handrail around the wall of the dining room in
the ranch house, and turned that into a roller skating rink.

We had lots of good times, but Granville Stuart was always very strict with his daughters. Even after Mary and I
were engaged, we couldn't hardly get out of the house alone
after dark. If we walked out so we could have a little talk
together, her father would come to the door and call out:
"Children, it's time to go to bed!" How sore it used to
make me!

Mary was always my favorite, though I paid more attention to her older sister Katie at first. When I came to the
ranch she was only fifteen, but I always called her my little
wife.

I laid over at the D H S that first winter, and I knew
what to do to make myself popular. I didn't just sit around
and eat the grub. I carried wood and water for the cook and
wiped his dishes, and did any other little jobs that come

along. About March, Percy Kennet, the foreman, said: "Say, I like your style." And he put me to work early helping to round up the horses. All the cow outfits turned out most of their horses after the fall roundup was over, only keeping up a few gentle ones to use in the winter. That meant a lot to do in the early spring, rounding them up and riding them so as to be ready when the cow work started.

Our roundup commenced in June, 1886, and that was where we shone. We were a famous outfit. You know Charlie Russell always give the cowpunchers the best of it in his pictures, and one time I asked him where he found all those good-looking cowhands he drew. He said: "Over at the D H S."

We were known among the other cowpunchers as the white shirt brigade. I guess you could lay that to the feminine influence. Our outfit branded at Fritz's Run corral about three miles from the ranch, and the girls would ride over to watch us. It was a great occasion for us, and so we would get all shaved up, put on our best clothes, and ride our top horses. And you would see damn fools like Teddy Blue and Perk Burnett wrastling calves and cutting ears, blood flying in every direction, down on the ground in the dusty old corral, with a white boiled shirt on, and twelve-dollar California pants. Light-gray ones, too. We were all hoping that when the branding was over, we'd get to ride home with one of the girls.

When I left there that spring to follow the other round-ups, Granville Stuart handed me a list of forty-two brands belonging to all the outfits on the Maginnis range, and I repped for those forty-two brands and had to keep all of them and all the earmarks in my head.

That was the spring that I first met Charlie Russell. The D H S roundup and the Moccasin roundup was working together that year, doubling up on each other's territory because they figured there had been a big drift. When we got back to the edge of the Moccasin territory, we found the Judith Basin roundup waiting for us, and for ten days the three roundups was together. After they got to Dog Creek, our crowd pulled back, but we left a rep wagon there and I stayed with it, and they put me to wrangling horses. Russell was doing the wrangling for the Judith Basin roundup, and that was how me and him got so thick. He would leave his horses on one side of the creek and I'd leave mine the other, and we'd get up there on top of a hill, and lay in the shade of our saddle horses, and augur[1] for hours. We talked about everything we'd ever knowed or done, and he told me all about Fort Benton, which I'd never been to, and I told him about my trips up the trail.

One day I rode down to Claggett, which was on the Missouri River at the mouth of the Judith River. A party of Assiniboine Sioux was just coming across the river on the ferry, seven lodges of them, and they was bent on a celebration. They had killed three bear in the Bear Paw Mountains, on the north side of the river, and they had sold the hides and meat to the captain of the steamboat *Rosebud* for seventy-five dollars, and they was going to spend it for grub and clothes and ammunition and whisky.

The fellow that had the ferry was rowing the Indians across in a little boat, and I sat down in the shade of a big cottonwood tree to watch them. Pretty soon along come a big Indian, and I said, "How," and he said, "How," and he sat down beside me. He knew a little English, and I knew some Sioux and some sign, and he had been drinking and wanted to talk. I asked him where they were going, and he

[1] Probably a corruption of "argue."

144

said they were going down the river with their women and just lay around, fishing and drinking whisky.

So we talked awhile about what they were going to do down there and then we got on the subject of the old days. I said: "You fellows used to have a pretty good time."

He said, "Yes," and then he described the way they used to live before the white man came. They would go down a creek and camp where there was good grass and water, run a bunch of buffalo down and skin them and get the meat— then when the grass got a little short, they would just move on to a place where there was new grass, and keep that up, no troubles or worries, and when one wife got old, they'd marry another one.

Coming back up Dog Creek, I met Russell. I said: "God, I wish I'd been a Sioux Indian a hundred years ago," and I told him the story.

He said: "Ted, there's a pair of us. They've been living in heaven for a thousand years, and we took it away from 'em for forty dollars a month."

That was the reason I liked Russell so much. We felt the same way about pretty nearly everything, and he could always see the funny side of things and so could I.

Another time I got talking to some of these Indians and one old fellow offered me his wife, for twenty-two dollars. This was not to keep, you understand, just a temporary arrangement. Twenty-two dollars was too high. A dollar and a half was more like it. Of course he made a big talk about her being his favorite wife and so forth, but that was all bull. Most of the Indian tribes was doing a regular business of that kind with the white men, and some of them, especially the Crows and Sioux, had got so low they would offer you their wives. But the way they did it in most of the

145

camps, they had special tepees for the purpose, and certain squaws that was just like sporting women among the whites. Only among the Indians it never seemed to hurt their chances for marrying afterwards.

The Gros Ventres, Crows, and Sioux, and I think the Blackfeet were all doing this kind of business. But never the Northern Cheyennes, nor the Pawnees, down in Nebraska. You couldn't touch one of their women unless you married her with a priest.

I tried hard to get a Cheyenne girl once. But she wouldn't even marry me. She was one of a big band of Cheyennes that was camped all over our range, from Armall's Creek to the Rosebud, in 1883. There was two lodges of them that came down to the F U F ranch, and I told the old man it was a good idea to treat them well and give them a little grub once in awhile, tea and coffee and sugar. They didn't have any too much of it.

For these were the Indians that put up that great fight in '78, when they broke out of the reservation down in Indian Territory where they had been sent for punishment after the Custer battle in '76. They broke out under Dull Knife and Little Wolf, and they fought their way clear up from Indian Territory to Tongue River in Montana, because they was dying like flies down there, dying for home. There was three hundred Indians, and less than a hundred of them was warriors, the rest women and old men and children. And with thirteen thousand troops out against them they fought their way across three railroads and five lines of defense, and they whipped everything they come to. And by God, half of them made it up here to Montana, and for a wonder they was allowed to stay. I tell you they was the bravest Indians on the plains—the Northern Cheyennes.

This girl I speak of was in one of their tepees that came

down and camped near the ranch, and oh, but she was a good-looking girl. It wasn't easy to see much of her. She was very modest. You had to hunt her. But she did come to the ranch house once or twice, for dinner, with the rest of them. You see, we put on kind of a party for them, cooked up some plum duff and so on; because two or three of us in the outfit was in Nebraska when they come through there like a prairie fire in '78, and we knew these Indians, what they were. We ought to know. They killed eighteen cowboys down there when they was making that break for home. They come pretty near getting me, too, but if I'd been in their place I'd have done the same.

One of the lodges that was camped on Armall's Creek belonged to an Indian named High Walking. He was one of the government's Cheyennes that were scouts with Miles during the Nez Percé campaign—because a lot of those Indians would fight with the government against their old enemies—and he could talk pretty good English. I used to sit and visit with him nights, in the tepee. You hear talk about Indians being dirty, and a lot of them are today, so it makes you sick sometimes to see them. But these modern reservation Indians are entirely different. Mrs. High Walking kept her lodge as neat and clean as any white woman I ever knew kept her house, and their kid was dressed like a little warrior. She was a manager, too. The Indians loved coffee, and they had very little of it, and I have seen Mrs. High Walking take six beans of coffee and pound it up for coffee for her and her husband.

The girl would be in the tepee nights, with the rest of them. I never had much chance to talk to her. She would just sit there with her head down and wouldn't say nothing. She didn't have to. You knew all you needed to know, just looking at her. I did try to make up to her a couple of times, but she give me to understand she didn't want a damn thing to do with me. She seemed a little bit freer when the men were not around. I think she was afraid of them. The Cheyennes were very strict with their women. They were one of the Indian tribes that would cut off a wife's nose if she was unfaithful, and I have seen them that way around the camps, with the tips of their noses sliced off. It was an awful thing to see.

I wanted this girl so much that I asked her if she'd marry me, but she wouldn't do that either. I asked her through old High Walking, and as I told him: "She's good enough for me."

Well, she was, or that was the way I felt about it at the time. And I wasn't the only one by a long way, because there was plenty of cowpunchers in that early day who were not ashamed to marry an Indian girl. You couldn't blame us. We were starving for the sight of a woman, and some of these young squaws were awful good-looking, with their fringed dresses of soft deer or antelope skin that hung just below their knees—that was all they wore, just the dress— and their beaded leggings and wide beaded belts. Oh, boy, but they looked good to us. But I was always that way. I always wanted a dark-eyed woman.

There is one thing more I want to say about these mixed marriages that used to take place in the early days. Those Indian women made wonderful wives. The greatest attraction in a woman, to an Indian, was obedience. They were taught that and they inherited it. Their husband's will was their law. Every white man I ever knew that was married to an Indian—like Granville Stuart—thought the world of them.

17

Scraps of Paper—
The Heroic Cheyennes—Dull Knife and Little Wolf—
Too Excited to Shoot Straight—
Little Wolf Wins Through

I was always different from the general run of the white men because I liked the Indians and could see their side of things. Well, no, not always. But from the time I was old enough to know the facts. After I got some sense in my head and saw the way things really was in that country, I was sorry for the Indians and ashamed of the deal they got at the hands of the white men. But, as my mother used to say when she saw how I took to their way of living, I was pretty nearly one of them anyway.

They can't show a place in history where the Indians ever broke a treaty. The white men always broke them because they always made a treaty they couldn't keep and knew they couldn't keep it. And that is something I know, not just the way you know a thing you have read about, but the way you know it when you have seen it, and it stays with you always like a picture in your mind.

I told you how, after I run away from home that time when I was eighteen, I took a beef herd up to the Pine Ridge Indian agency in northwestern Nebraska. The herd was trailed up from Texas by Millett and Mabry under contract to the government, and they issued them to the Sioux Indians as part of a big celebration over signing another treaty, where the Indians ceded some more of their country. They drawed up the treaty fixing the new boundaries for the reservation, which had been cut down twice already, and they got some of these coffee-coolers[1] to consent to it, and they had General Miles there with two thousand soldiers. Afterwards they issued out the herd of beef.

This was in November, 1878. After we delivered the beef up there, we heard about the big doings at the agency, and we went inside to watch what was going on. I remember there was an old fellow with a long white beard who sat in the middle, with a table in front of him; he must have been the Indian commissioner or a special government agent. General Miles was on one side of him and the interpreters on the other, and the Indians squatted in a semicircle on the ground. Each chief had his little speech to make before he put his mark to the treaty, and each one of them got up and talked, and what he said was interpreted to the commissioner, all with the most perfect decorum.

And the last one to get up was this chief they called John Grass. He was a young fellow, tall and fine-looking, and finely educated. He had a *parflêche* full of papers, and he kept pulling them out and reading from them, in English. They gave the history of all the government's treaties with the Sioux. The first was the one they made after the big raids in Minnesota in '62. They made a treaty then putting all the Sioux west of the Mississippi and promising them that the land would be theirs "for all time to come."

Then John Grass pulled out another paper, and the government had moved them again, and cut the reservation down again. This time they moved them west of the Missouri. They were to have the Yellowstone River on the north, the Big Horn Mountains on the west, and the Platte

1 Yes-men among the Indians who would do anything for a cup of coffee.

River on the south, and again they promised them that the land would be theirs "for all time to come."

"And now," he said, "you want the Black Hills." He said: "How would you like it if people go and take the land where you bury your dead?" He said: "I have been to Carlisle. I have as good an education as the white man will give me. And I still do not understand these treaties. I would ask some of you gentlemen to tell me what those words mean, 'For all time to come.' "

I was standing at the back of the room with the other cowpunchers listening to all this, and I thought the deal was all right at the time. I don't think so now. Not that I was ever a special friend of the Sioux. Of all the Indians, the ones I admired the most were the Northern Cheyennes. That time they broke out in Oklahoma and fought their way north to this country up here was the greatest fight ever put up by any bunch of Indians in all history. And they were 100 per cent in the right all the time, because they were fighting to get back to their own country, that had been theirs for more years than the oldest Indian could remember. One U. S. Army officer who was out against them said it was the "greatest national movement ever made by any people since the Greeks marched to the sea."

You can read about it in a very few books, the best account being in *Reminiscences of a Ranchman* by Edgar Beecher Bronson, in the chapter called "A Finish Fight for a Birthright." But except for that book and perhaps one or two others, you will seldom hear anything about the great fight made by Dull Knife and Little Wolf in '78, because the white man is such a damn poor loser he does not talk about the times when the Indians were victorious. Even the Custer fight is no exception to this statement, because, while the Indians cleaned up on Custer at the Little Big Horn, the government sent out more troops and cleaned up on the Indians later in that same year, 1876.

It was after the campaign in the fall of 1876 that Dull Knife and his tribe were sent down to Fort Reno in Indian Territory, or the Nations as it was called at that time. That is a hot, low-lying country, and they was used to the high plains. All through 1877 and the first half of 1878 they sickened and died. They begged the government to let them come back to their own home, but this was refused. In September, 1878, the whole tribe jumped the reservation and headed north. Going up through Kansas, they fought five battles in less than three weeks and fought the soldiers off every time, and where they didn't fight, they slipped through and kept on going, and the United States Army couldn't stop them.

They crossed the Kansas Pacific Railroad and burned down some houses near Dodge City, after they'd whipped two companies of cavalry first. They crossed the Union Pacific half a mile east of Ogallala. And, boy, those Indians were traveling. They were making seventy miles a day with women and children, and raiding on the cow outfits as they went along, to get fresh horses. They run onto a band of cowboys at the forks of Republican River and killed eighteen of them, and everybody else that was in the country got out of the way. I know I run at least a hundred miles.

When they got up to the North Platte River, Bill Paxton's ranch was on their line of march, and they stole some of his horses. From the way Bill talked about it he thought Johnny Stringfellow ought to have stood them off, or else followed them up and got back the horses. String told me about it. He said: "Bill Paxton wanted to know why I didn't go after them Indians. I told him I hadn't lost no Cheyennes."

They killed quite a few people and burned some ranches, but you couldn't blame them for that because they were only savages and were fighting for their freedom like savages. On all that long march they didn't do but one really bad thing. I did hear that they come across a lonely schoolhouse, and some of them took the teacher and one of the older girl pupils and abused them. They both got well and I believe got married afterwards. Sixty years is a long time to remember all the details of a thing like that and I am not sure this is right. But I believe it was done by a small bunch of young bucks who were raiding out from the main bunch. The Cheyennes were very moral Indians, and it was not like them to do a thing like that as a rule. The Apaches was the worst ones for that kind of stuff.

All this happened in October, after I left home and just before I went up to the Pine Ridge agency with that beef herd. I was up on the North Platte by this time, when the Indians got up there, a posse went out to chase them, and I was with the posse. They was scattered out in bunches of fifteen or twenty, raiding on the different ranches while the main bunch kept pushing on, and this band that we were following dropped back and stood us off, in an arroyo. I was lying down behind a little buck brush, trying to get a shot at an Indian, and one of them saw me and took a shot at me, and it kicked up the dust in my face. I can shiver yet when I think of it.

There was an Indian in this bunch they called Brave Wolf, who was a great warrior. They claim he danced thirteen dried buffalo heads off him before he started from the reservation, to make his medicine strong. And he got up there in the arroyo in front of us, all painted up, and he did a war dance to prove we couldn't kill him. He was prancing around out there, going "Hi-ya, hi-ya," with sixteen of us shooting at him and all too excited to hit him, until finally somebody got him through the head. They picked him up by the arms and dragged him over the hills. We let them go. We had got our bellyful of Cheyennes.

And that was all I saw of them until I got up to Montana in '83 and they was here. But I heard the rest of the story from Hank Thompson, who was a government scout up at Fort Keogh for years, and knew the Cheyennes very well and was married to a Cheyenne woman. And I also heard about it from some of the Indians who made the trip, especially Wolf Robe and High Walking. When they got up into the sand hills of western Nebraska, they run out of cow outfits, so they run out of horses. They knew they would never make it the way they were going, so Dull Knife and Little Wolf decided to separate. Little Wolf, the young chief, was to take the fighting men and most of the ammunition and the best horses, and try to get through. Dull Knife took the old men and women and children, and just a few warriors.

The country was full of soldiers patrolling up and down, ready to head them off. So Little Wolf and his band went up and showed themselves on top of a high hill, and the soldiers saw them and surrounded the hill in the night and thought they had got them. When morning come, there wasn't an Indian—they was so much smarter than the troops at that kind of game. But that move by Little Wolf gave Dull Knife the only chance he had, and he and his women and his old men sneaked off into the brush down on White River. The soldiers captured them there a few days later and took them to Fort Robinson. They were out of ammunition, they were starving, they didn't have a horse that could travel. Of course, when they were taken prisoner, the soldiers took all their weapons away, but in spite of everything those Indians managed to take a few guns apart and hide them under the squaws' dresses, and a few small knives, and when they got to the fort they hid them under the floor boards of the guardhouse.

And the post commander was going to send them back to the reservation down in Oklahoma, marching overland through that terrible below-zero weather, and these Indians had no clothes, they were naked, they would have froze to death. So Dull Knife refused to go. So that fool of a commander ordered their rations cut off because they were disobedient, and for three days they were in the guardhouse with nothing to eat, just swaying back and forth and singing their war chants; and the third night they took their few poor weapons that they had hid and killed a couple of sentries and made a break for the hills. They had nothing to fight with, nothing, only sticks and a few guns and a few knives, but they fought anyway, women too; and one man who was there tells of seeing a big six-foot warrior dying, with a little three-inch skinning knife in his hand. That was all he had. Pretty nearly the whole band died fighting, women and all.

But Little Wolf and his followers won out, and that is one of the miracles of Indian history. They got clear up here almost to Tongue River, when General Miles come down from Fort Keogh with a big body of troops and demanded their surrender. They said no, they would never surrender. They said that before they would go back to the reservation in Oklahoma, they would kill each other with their knives. But then they told him that if the government would let them stay up here in their old country on Tongue River, they would lay down their arms and be good Indians and never make any more trouble. Miles knew it was a question of that, or else he would have to massacre these Indians and lose a lot of men himself, so he agreed.

And for a wonder the government backed him up, instead of double-crossing him and making a liar out of him the way they done when Chief Joseph surrendered after the Nez Percé campaign. And so Miles' word was not broken, and the Indians was allowed to stay and keep their victory.

And that is the whole story of why the Northern Cheyennes were up here when I came to this country in '83, and why they are here today. They have a little bit of a reservation on Tongue River and the Rosebud, not half as big as the reservation next to it that the government gave the Crows. But the Crows were smart; they fought on the government side in the seventies. And so the Crows are well off; they drive cars and run race horses, but nobody ever heard of a Cheyenne with a race horse. They are too poor.

But this reservation they are living on today is their country that they fought for in '78, and half of them died. In the old days, no matter how far they went on their hunting parties, they would always come back to Tongue River to winter. It was home to them. And no wonder. It is a beautiful country, well watered, with high hills and big yellow pines scattered over them, and grass everywhere, and lots of shelter. They were used to this, and that is why when they had to go down to that low, flat Oklahoma country they took sick and died.

But a lot more things happened even after they were allowed to stay up here in '78. Because wherever Indians and white men come together there is bound to be trouble, or there was until the Indians was completely broken. There was trouble with the Cheyennes up here in the season of '83–'84, and I was mixed up in it though it was more or less against my will.

18

Cheyenne Outbreak of '84—
"We Are Even"—In Front of a Tepee—
Pine Is My Indian—
"C Co 7 Cav"—Nobody Will Ever See It Again

It was just about the time of the big chinook that came in March of '84, and a few snowdrifts still showed up, when a Cheyenne named Black Wolf and his immediate family of seven lodges came over from Tongue River to the Rosebud on a visit to the other Indians. They camped at the mouth of Lame Deer Creek, near where two partners named Zook and Alderson had a ranch. One day the chief, Black Wolf, went up to this ranch by himself, and the boys gave him dinner. There was just two of them there at the time, a fellow named Sawney Tolliver, from Kentucky originally, and another one whose name I don't remember.

After Black Wolf had filled up, like an Indian would, he walked out and sat down in the sun on some poles, and he went to sleep. He had an old black stovepipe hat on, and this Tolliver stood at the door of the ranch house and said to the other fellow: "I'll bet you a dollar I can shoot a hole through his hat without hitting his head."

The fellow took him up, and Tolliver threw down on the Indian, and he just creased him along his scalp. You could lay your finger in the mark. It knocked him out and they thought they had killed him. So they got on their horses and rode to the next ranch to get help, because they expected to have hell with the Indians, and they expected right. When they got back to the ranch with their reinforcements, Black Wolf was gone. But they knew the Indians would be coming just the same, and pretty soon they come and commenced shooting. When the other cowboys saw how many Indians there was, they just stampeded off, because they had no stomach for the business anyhow. It was a damn fool trick that caused the trouble. Tolliver left, too, quit the country. If he'd been caught, he'd have gone to jail, you bet, and he knew it. The soldiers would have seen to that.

The Indians went to work and burnt the house down, and shot the dog, and then they quit right there. Hank Thompson told me that in talking about it afterwards they put their two forefingers together, which is the sign meaning "We are even." Some people claim that they stole some provisions out of the house, coffee and so on, and that the stuff was found in their tepees after they surrendered. I don't know, I didn't go in the tepees. My sympathies was with the Indians.

The cowboys who ran away got word to the soldiers and to the sheriff in Miles City that the Cheyennes had broke out. The first we knew of it over at the F U F was when my friend Billy Smith, the stock inspector, who was in charge of the sheriff's posse, turned up at the ranch calling for help to arrest the Indians and protect a couple of white families that were in danger at the mouth of Lame Deer. By this time it was two days after the shooting, because it was one long day's ride of ninety or a hundred miles to Miles City, and another one to the F U F. We ate dinner and got on our horses, and along about 2:00 A.M., we got to one of these white families at the mouth of Lame Deer, where the posse was supposed to rendezvous. We found them all up and scared to death—though the Indians hadn't done a damn

thing yet, only burn down the house where their man had
been shot. It was lucky he didn't die, or there would have
been hell.

Next day the posse divided, and fourteen of us, keeping
this side of the Rosebud, rode away around and tied our
horses in some brush, left two men with them, and after
dark crawled up to where we were in between the Rosebud
and the Indian camp. It makes me shiver yet when I think

of the chance we took. There was no shelter whatever. We were right up against a high cut bank, with the river running fast and churning ice below us, so there was no way out in that direction. The tepees were about seventy-five yards in front of us and a bright moon was shining. Some of the others said the Indians were asleep. My God, I could look into the tepee right opposite me and see the moonlight shining off the barrel of his gun—because they always polish off that black stuff—and I imagined I could see the hole at the end of the barrel, and it followed me everywhere.

At daylight Hank Thompson and the deputy from Miles City rode into the Indian camp, and believe me that was a brave thing to do. But the Indians liked Hank and trusted him completely. He called to Black Wolf in Cheyenne who they were, and Black Wolf invited them into his tepee and called all the other warriors into council. That's when they told Hank they were even. They hadn't done nothing wrong in their estimation.

The old fellow, Black Wolf, was very tall and dignified, and he had a great big piece of buffalo manure tied on his head over the wound. Hank told them they were surrounded and asked them to surrender, and they all talked and argued. One Indian, Howling Wolf, was determined to fight, not surrender, and he kept tongue-lashing the others; he was all hate, and the white men knew he was dangerous and they was watching him.

Out on the bank we could hear the talking going on, but we couldn't hear what they said or which way it was going until all of a sudden Hank Thompson's voice rang out clear, in English, speaking to Louis King. He said: "If anything starts, get that Indian that's doing the talking."

And Louis said: "I'll get him right between the eyes."

We expected any second to hear the shooting start, after that, and if it had started, God help us. I figure they would have got at least six of us outside, beside the two in the tepee. And we laid there cramped and shivering in the early morning cold—we had been there three hours already—and we waited. And we waited some more. During the World War I read about men going over the top, and I know what it is like. It's the waiting that gets you. You feel your whole self go down in your boots, and you feel the gun in your hand—and then you wait another half hour.

And all the time Hank Thompson was talking, talking in

Cheyenne, explaining things to the Indians and promising that they would get a square deal if they surrendered. And after awhile Black Wolf, who was the subchief at the head of this little bunch, agreed. And the Indians all walked out, thirteen of them, and gave up their guns. They built a big fire then, and we came in and surrounded them and searched them for knives. All but one young brave named Pine had given them up, and he put up a big fight for his knife, which he had in his breech clout, and they couldn't get it away from him. But Black Wolf made him give it up. They're obedient in all things to the chief.

We had an awful narrow squeak in that camp, even after the surrender. When we came in and surrounded them, we didn't bother the women, naturally. It was breakfast time and they were busy around the camp, going back and forth to the river for water. And four or five would do down to the river, and three or four would come back. And three would go down, and two would come back. . . . And they kept that up until there was only one old woman left in that camp. There was a trail that led around through some brush, on the top of the cut bank, and they was crawling along that trail on their hands and knees, going to get word to the whole tribe, which was camped only six miles away.[1]

One of our posse happened to see the head and shoulders of one squaw, as she crawled along where the trail went out of the brush a little way, and that woke him up. He took one look around the camp and yelled: "Where the hell's all them women?" After that they rounded them up and brought them back. There was two or three hundred Indians in that

[1] Why were all the women trying to make their getaway, when one alone could have taken word to the tribe? I asked Mr. Abbott this, and he pointed out that in numerous instances atrocities had been committed by white soldiers on Indian women and children. All the Indians knew of these occurrences, and they were afraid for their lives.

bunch six miles away, and if those women had gotten through to them, it would have been the end of us.

After we had disarmed the Indians, we marched them down to Gaffney's house, that was one of the white families I mentioned at the mouth of Lame Deer. And there I was sworn in as a special deputy, on account of Billy Smith knowing me before. Billy Smith was in charge of the posse. We got our breakfast down there, and Mrs. Gaffney done the cooking for all of us and the Indians, too. After breakfast we loaded the Indians in a wagon and started off for Miles City, where they were to be tried.

There was a lot of things happened in that Indian camp after I left that I only know about through hearsay. Frank Abbott, who came over with the rest of us from the F U F, says there was a young squaw, Pine's squaw, that had only been married two weeks, and she tried to follow her husband, and he says he has always been sorry for the way they had to treat her to make her go back. But he was disgusted to beat everything with the whole affair, and we was all disgusted when we found out what it was all about, and what danger we had been in for a damn fool trick. Frank says this squaw tried to go to Miles City, while the Indians were in prison before the trial, and was drowned crossing Tongue River. But I couldn't say as to that, because I never heard anything more about it.

We got down to Carpenter and Robinson's ranch just before dark, and there we heard that the Tollivers hadn't made enough trouble yet, because Sawney Tolliver's brother, Brownie, had said he was going to follow us with a bunch of men and going to shoot the Indians in the wagon. Unarmed Indians. Sawney was in Wyoming by this time. Billy Smith left word at the ranch that if anybody followed us and tried to meddle with the Indians, we would shoot them down like dogs. Those Indians had surrendered without firing a shot.

And that wasn't the only reason that we felt as we did. There was only six of us in the posse that took them to Miles City, and if those thirteen Indians had all give a yell and jumped for it out of the wagon, in the night, we'd never have hit a one of them. But they'd given their word. Or Black Wolf had, and what he said went for the rest of them. They always looked to the chief.

In the meanwhile there was still this main bunch of two or three hundred Indians only six miles up from the mouth of Lame Deer, and they'd have jumped the whole United States Army if their chief had given the word. But he didn't give the word. And there again we owed everything to the honor of an Indian.

For on our way to Carpenter and Robinson's that afternoon we saw this one tepee, out from the side of the road. It was the tepee of Little Wolf, the war chief of all the Cheyennes, who was camped out there by himself. And Hank Thompson rode over to him and begged and pleaded with him to give his word that he would stay where he was for another twenty-four hours instead of going in to join his tribe. This would give us a chance to get to Miles City. For Little Wolf was the Cheyennes' great chief, who had led them up here in '78, and they would not move without him.

He finally promised to stay where he was, and he kept his promise, and that saved all our lives. He was a wise leader as well as a great fighter, Little Wolf was, and I believe he was wise enough not to want any more trouble with the white man. He had had a plenty of it, and I believe he knew that the white man was bound to win in the end.

We traveled all that night, the six of us and the Indians. I kept going to sleep in the saddle, because it was the second night for me, and I remember Billy Smith jerking my horse's head up when he went to grazing on me. About daybreak we got to Rosebud station on the Northern Pacific, and we waited there for the train to take us to Miles City. And there I claimed this young Indian, Pine, that wouldn't give up his knife, for my Indian, my friend, and I looked after him as best I could. He was one of the best-looking Indians I ever saw, six feet, one or two inches tall and as straight as a string. And he was brave—he fought for his knife—and I was sure stuck on him.

We all ate there, while we was waiting for the train, and I handed Pine the grub and water first, but he always handed them up to the chief—everything for the chief. And after they had eaten they all wrapped up in their blankets and laid down on their stomachs and went to sleep. And so did I—right beside Pine.

By and by the train came, and we all got on it and went to Miles City. The whole town was out to see us come in with the Indians. At the station we loaded them all in a bus, to take them to the jail at the fort, and I was on top of the bus, so everybody thought I was the cowboy that done the shooting. There was a very popular demi-mondaine by the name of Willie Johnson, who was running Kit Hardiman's honky-tonk, as I have mentioned before, and I remember she came to the door of the house and hollered: "Stay with it, Blue! Don't you weaken!"

When we turned the Indians over to the authorities at Fort Keogh, Major Logan, the commanding officer, was as sore as a boil. He said, here was the Indians, but where was the fellow that started the trouble? And when they told him he was out of the country by that time, Major Logan said the posse was a hell of an outfit and gave us the devil, until, as Billy Smith said afterwards, if he'd had one more word out of him, he'd have hit him over the head with his six-shooter.

I'll tell you something about soldiers. At the first news of the outbreak they started a company of them from Fort Keogh, with a cannon. And when we got up to Miles City with the Indians, these soldiers had gone just forty miles, which was less than half the distance to the scene of the trouble, in the same time it took the sheriff's posse to go clear down to the mouth of Lame Deer and get the Indians and get back. But that's the way they always was in the army —had to go by West Point regulations; had to build their campfire in a certain position from the tent regardless of the way the wind was blowing. They was no earthly good on the frontier.

Well, the thirteen Indians was shut up under guard, and the next morning the whole Cheyenne tribe rode into Miles City. The people were scared to death. They didn't know what was going to happen. But the Indian prisoners had been guaranteed a fair trial, and Hank Thompson was among the Cheyennes all the time, talking to them like a Dutch uncle. So nothing happened. They finally fixed it all up. Four of the Indians pled guilty to burning the ranch house and got a year apiece in the pen, and they turned the rest loose. One of them died up there of grief.

While they were all in jail, I went to see Pine every day, and took him presents of tailor-made cigarettes and candy and stuff. And I told him I'd get him out of it, and luckily he did get out of it, and he was my friend for life. The last day he took a silver ring off his finger and gave it to me. The ring had a little shield, and on the shield it said "C Co 7 Cav." That was Tom Custer's company, and Pine took it off the finger of one of Tom Custer's soldiers at the fight, and he was in that fight when he was not yet fourteen years old.[2] The ring was too small for me, and I wore it around my neck for years, but in the end somebody got away with it.

That business at the mouth of Lame Deer opened my eyes to a lot of things about the Indians. I had it in for them before that, but it was due to ignorance. I had seen a lot of them, but I never associated with them the way I did after I got up to Montana. From that time I was on their side, because I saw that when trouble started, more often than not it was the white man's fault.

Not three months after the so-called outbreak I have been telling about, there was another mix-up with the Cheyennes, and it started in the very same outfit—Zook and Alderson. After the Indians burned their ranch on Lame Deer, they moved the outfit, and instead of staying away from these Indians they moved right up into the thick of them, on Hanging Woman, which is another creek in the Tongue River country. It almost seemed like they were looking for trouble; yet that couldn't have been true, because Alderson and his partner were both nice fellows and I believe they were away, both times, when the trouble occurred.

It was during the spring roundup, and they were all out with the roundup except a cowboy named Packsaddle Jack and a couple of others, who were breaking horses at the ranch. Packsaddle Jack was bringing in his horses, early one morning, and there was a Cheyenne named Iron Shirt who had a little garden near there—corn and pumpkins and stuff. And Packsaddle drove his horses right over the Indian's garden, and when the Indian come out and objected, Packsaddle shot him in the arm.

[2] Pine is still living on the Tongue River Reservation and he and Mr. Abbott renewed their acquaintance in the summer of 1938.

Well, there was a lot of riding around and excitement, the same story all over again. Except that some of the cow-punchers had got their bellyful by this time. And when a couple of fellows from Zook and Alderson's rode over to the roundup and asked for men to help defend the ranch, Jesse Garland, the roundup captain, told them to go to hell. He said: "You got us into one jackpot this spring, and I won't allow a man to leave this roundup."

It all blew over. The Cheyennes knew they were beaten, and they were trying to keep the peace. Packsaddle Jack was tried in Miles City that fall and acquitted. And the rest of us weren't going against those fighting Indians on account of any more damned foolishness like that.

But it led to more and still more trouble. Several white men were found dead. Then another white man got killed by two young Indians in a fuss over a cow, which he said they had butchered, and I don't doubt they had. The chief sent word for them to come in, as the tribe would get into trouble for it, and he was going to punish them. They sent word back that they would come, but in their own way.

And they went up on top of a hill, and they sang their death songs, and painted themselves, and braided their horses' manes. And then they rode down from the hill, just the two of them, and charged two companies of soldiers that were sent out to arrest them. Which shows you the desperate courage of those Cheyennes.

I forgot to tell you about one thing that happened that morning on the Rosebud. While we were lying out there in the grass, half froze and waiting for all hell to break loose out of that tepee, I saw an old Indian go up a hill and pray to the sun. It was just coming up, and the top of the hill was red with it, and we were down there shivering in the shadow. And he was away off on the hill, and he held up his arms, and oh, God, but did he talk to the Great Spirit about the wrongs the white man had done to his people. I never have heard such a voice. It must have carried a couple of miles.

I have noticed that what you see when you are cold and scared is what you remember, and that is a sight I will never forget. I am glad that I saw it. Because nobody will ever see it again.

19

The Hard Winter—Pike Landusky—Sixty Below—
"Fair, Fair, with Golden Hair"—
"You Smell like an Old Indian"—A Frozen Wilderness—
Deep Snow and Indian Whisky—Spring at Last

In 1886 the only new range left in Montana was north of
the Missouri River, on the Blackfoot reservation. Where
Granville Stuart had come into a virgin country in 1880,
with plenty of long grass for his cattle and hostile Indians
his only neighbors, here was the condition in the Judith
Basin six years later. The buffalo was all gone, there was a
town at Fort Maginnis and another one at Maiden, eight
miles up toward the Judith Mountains; the Northern Pacific Railroad was running through central Montana, and
the settlers had come in so thick they was crowding the cattlemen everywhere. But there was still about a hundred
miles of good grass between the Missouri and Milk River,
and Granville Stuart got permission from the government
to move his cattle up there.

When I got back from the beef roundup that fall, they
put me to work with the trail herds they were taking up
north of the Missouri, and I helped take two herds across.
We had an awful time with the second one. Winter set in
early, with a big storm and freeze in November that lasted
two solid days and nights. We got all ready to cross them
on the ice, and we had a trail of dirt laid over it so they
wouldn't slip, when there come a thaw and the ice broke

up. We all quit then and went back to the ranch, and it was almost a month before the river froze over again so we could get them across. In the meanwhile a lot of them drifted back on the range, and we never did get them that winter. When spring came, most of the cattle on both sides of the river were dead.

That winter I rode with Pike Landusky between the Missouri River and Milk River. We took a pack outfit and camped out nearly all winter around the Little Rocky Mountains. Granville Stuart sent us up there to look out for rustlers and Indians and see that they did not kill beef, and also to hold the cattle back from going too far north. That was the hard winter and we had an awful time, but we never accomplished a thing, and there was no real reason for sending us. Nobody but us was moving in that kind of weather. The rustlers was all holed up.

Granville Stuart picked Pike because he was known as a hard man and a fighter and looked like the right man for the job. He had been around in that country more than twenty years, trapping, wolfing, prospecting, cutting wood for the steamboats, and trading with the Indians. His real name was Powell Landusky, and he said he was half Polish and half French, but he was always called Pike because he came from Pike County, Missouri. He was a great big man, six feet, one inch tall, 190 pounds in weight, and a dead shot. One side of his jaw was missing, because he got shot in a row with some Blackfeet when he was running an Indian trading post down on Flatwillow in the seventies. They was taking him to Reed's Fort for treatment after the fight, but the wound pained him so much that he tore out a piece of that shattered jawbone, with a couple of teeth attached and threw it away. It marked him for life, and when the weather got cold he would slobber out of that side of his face.

172

The Hard Winter

He was famous for his violent temper. An old partner of his, by the name of John Wirt, told me about the time Pike ran amuck with some Indians one winter when the two of them was hunting together near the mouth of the Mussel-shell. This was in 1869, and the Indians were bad there. Along about the middle of the winter Pike and his partner went up to Carroll to get more ammunition and grub. When they got back down the river they met a big party of Brûlé Sioux, stripped to fight. The chief told them where to camp and told them to stay there; in other words they were captives, although the Indians didn't bother to take their guns away because they were so outnumbered.

All this happened at their old camp, where they were before they went up to Carroll. The Indians broke into everything. They found out where their furs were cached, that had cost them a winter's trapping, and they took their lion skins and made headdresses out of them, and they found some red flannel drawers of Pike's and made nightcaps out of those. And by and by Pike got sore. When an Indian reached over and grabbed a piece of meat he was cooking, Pike hit him over the head with the frying pan, and then he jumped on him and kicked hell out of him, and then he tore his breechcloth off and slapped it in his face. That is the deadliest insult you can give an Indian. Poor old John Wirt was just standing there—because it wouldn't have done a bit of good to run—and the only thing he could think of was to keep on saying, "Washtay—washtay," which is the Indian word for "good"—meaning Pike was a good man and not to pay no attention to him.

In the meantime Pike had grabbed his gun and run and poked it in an Indian's belly, and then charged another man, and the Indian was making the sign for "crazy." They won't touch a crazy person. Afterwards they gave him sixteen horses they had stolen from the Crows. But Pike never made peace with them, and to the day of his death he hated the Sioux. Three years later he met the Indian who stole his meat; Pike was trapping with another fellow and the Indian was with a little party, just three or four of them; and Pike killed this Indian and cut out his bladder and made a tobacco pouch of it, and I smoked out of that pouch that winter on the Missouri.

I thought Pike was kind of loading me when he told me the story, but John Wirt told me the same thing later, and Johnny Wirt was a different kind of a character altogether —a very cool-headed, brave man. And I know myself what a maniac Pike was when he got in one of his rages, because I saw him charge a bunch of Gros Ventres, only it wasn't as serious as that other time because there wasn't so many Indians. It was the end of that winter, when the chinook come, and a party of them went by the cabin. Mrs. Pike was going to have a baby, and one of the Indians noticed it and made the sign. Well, you know that sort of thing don't mean nothing to an Indian. But she ran to Pike and told him the Indian had insulted her, and he went after them like a crazy man, kicking and cussing and threatening them with his gun, while I sat there on my horse like a damned fool.

He was ferocious, that Pike. When he got mad he was blind. But after he got among cowpunchers and got to calling them son of a bitch he got his quietus, because they wouldn't stand for being cussed like that. He was shot and killed by "Kid" Curry in the town of Landusky, about 1894.

I always got along with him all right. He was a good partner, because he had been on the frontier a long time and knew how to take advantage of everything. He used to carry pine splinters soaked in coal oil for starting fires— you'd touch a match to them, and they would flare right up. Another trick he taught me was how to ward off snow blindness, though I didn't pay attention to him in time. There was snow on the ground from one end of that winter to the other and the glare was terrible. Pike cut out the black lining out of his coat and made a mask out of it, with holes for the eyes. I used to laugh at him for it. He said: "Christ Jesus! When you get her, you'll know her!" And I got her, the very next year. I went snow-blind and had to lie in bed for five days with salt poultices over my eyes, not able to sleep or eat or think from the pain.

Another thing he told me was: "You've got to dress so if you break your leg and have to lay out on the prairie you won't freeze to death." So here were the clothes I wore. I wore two pairs of wool socks, a pair of moccasins, a pair of Dutch socks that came up to the knees, a pair of government overshoes, two suits of heavy underwear, pants, overalls, chaps, and a big heavy shirt. I got a pair of woman's stockings and cut the feet out and made sleeves. I wore wool gloves, and great big heavy mittens, a blanket-lined sourdough overcoat, and a great big sealskin cap.

That way I kept warm enough. But not any too warm. For that was the celebrated winter of '86–'87 that broke the back of the range cattle business. In Wyoming and Montana the settlers had run all the big outfits off the plains, so they had moved up close to the mountains, causing the range to be overstocked. Then, too, the summer had been very dry, so what grass we had was eaten off before the first snow fell. In November we had several snowstorms, and I saw the first white owls I have ever seen. The Indians said they were a bad sign, heap snow coming, very cold, and they sure hit it right.

We had two weeks of nice weather just before Christmas. But on Christmas Eve it started to storm and never really let up for sixty days. It got colder and colder. I have a cutting from the post paper at Fort Keogh that reads that on January 14 it was sixty below zero at that place and snow two feet deep. The latter part of January it started a chinook —just enough to melt the snow on top. But it turned cold, and on February 3 and 4 the worst blizzard I ever saw set in. The snow crusted and it was hell without the heat.

The cattle stood it fairly well for thirty days. When the chinook started in January, I wrote to Granville Stuart, telling him I thought the loss would not be over 10 per cent. In ten days I know it was 75 per cent. The cattle drifted down on all the rivers, and untold thousands went down the air holes. On the Missouri we lost I don't know how many that way. They would walk out on the ice, and the ones behind would push the front ones in. The cowpunchers worked like slaves to move them back in the hills, but as all the outfits cut their forces down every winter, they were shorthanded. No one knows how they worked but themselves. They saved thousands of cattle. Think of riding all day in a blinding snowstorm, the temperature fifty and sixty below zero, and no dinner. You'd get one bunch of cattle up the hill and another one would be coming down behind you, and it was all so slow, plunging after them through the deep snow that way; you'd have to fight every step of the road. The horses' feet were cut and bleeding from the heavy crust, and the cattle had the hair and hide wore off their legs to the knees and hocks. It was surely hell to see big four-year-old steers just able to stagger along. It was the same all over Wyoming, Montana, and Colorado, western Nebraska, and western Kansas.

Pike had a cabin right close to the Rockies where he lived with his wife and family. Mrs. Pike was a French-woman from Louisiana, and as far as I know she was the only white woman in that country, because north of the river was all Blackfoot reservation at that time. She and five children had left her husband and married Pike in Maiden, Montana, a few years back, and she had two children by Pike. He was a good provider and very good to the whole family while I was there. She was a good housekeeper and a real nice little woman when she wasn't stirred up about something, and the only human being I ever met who was a match for Pike.

I lived with him that winter and the company paid him for my keep, but we was riding most of the time. I rode Grant, Mr. Stuart's old war horse, and one of the best horses I ever had my saddle on. December 24, we left our camp at the foot of the mountains and started home to Pike's for Christmas. I remember it was a beautiful day, clear and sunny, and as we rode along Pike kept showing me the different landmarks. At sundown we camped close to Tucker's cabin at the north end of the Little Rockies, expecting to be home in time for Christmas dinner the next day. But after dark it began to snow.

We made our beds down and Pike got in, but I sat by the campfire smoking and watching the snowflakes fall around me. That fall while we was shipping beef on the Northern Pacific I heard a girl singing a song at a dance hall in Junction; all I could remember was the tune and a line or two, that went: "Fair, fair with golden hair, Sang a fond mother while weeping." So I kept singing that over and over, till all at once Pike raised up on his elbow and roared out: "Christ Jesus! Can't you let her weep?" Then I taken off my overshoes and went to bed.

Next day the storm was so bad we didn't try to make it home, but rode over to John Healy's ranch on Lodge Pole because it was nearer. We found three men there, so we put

our horses in by a haystack and all cooked a Christmas dinner of deer meat and son-of-a-gun-in-a-sack (plum duff). We stayed there two days, but the storm kept getting worse, so we pulled out for home December 27. Healy's cabin was in a sheltered place, but when we got over the hill the wind and snow hit us so hard we could not see fifty feet ahead or hardly breathe. We tried to make Tucker's cabin again but missed it. That night we rode into a narrow canyon where we were out of the wind, but we got off our horses in snow up to our waist. We built a fire and made coffee, and held our meat on sticks until it thawed out, and ate it hot and raw. We never took the bridles off the horses, because there was nothing for them to eat.

Next morning we lit out for home and it was a fight for life. We had to ride sideways to the wind, and horses hate that. The wind blew the breath right out of our bodies and the snow cut like a knife. We got home nearly all in. We got off our horses and started to unpack, but the ropes were froze and our fingers so numb we could hardly untie them; when Mrs. Landusky run out of the house and begun giving us hell. She said: Where was we; and why didn't we come home; and this was a fine Christmas for her, with Indians all around and her alone here with all these children; and she had cooked us a big dinner, and so on and so forth. Pike never said a word at first, while she kept on calling us everything she could lay her tongue to because we didn't come home to Christmas dinner, when we like to have froze to death in that awful blizzard and it was a wonder we ever got there. And finally he turned to me and he says: "Christ Jesus! She was sure in the lead when tongues was give out."

And I laughed till I fell over in the snow.

From Pike's cabin in good weather you could see across the Missouri, straight south to the Judith Mountains and Black Butte, which was home to me because Mary was there. But there was very few days when you could see it, because of the snow and frost fog. And besides I wasn't there but very little. I was riding around with Pike and the pack outfit, most of that terrible winter. We camped in coulees, digging out the drifts and building our fires on top of the snow, and as I wrote Granville Stuart when I told him I wasn't going back to that country, the drifts were ninety feet deep. You know what the Indians say: "Indian make little fire, sit close, white man make big fire, sit back." Well, we made big fires and set close too, and when I came home to the D H S at the end of that winter I smelled so strong of smoke that the girls ordered me out of the house. They told me: "You smell like an old Indian"—or an old smoked fish, I forget which.

After Christmas, Pike and me made a trip to Milk River looking for rustlers, though there wasn't any rustlers. North of the Little Rockies is a great big plain where the wind sweeps down from the north, and there is no brush and no shelter of any kind except coulees, and you couldn't find those on account of the snow; and we come across it all the way to Milk River, where Malta is now, more than a week both ways, and we never saw a living soul. The Indians was all at the agencies, eating good grub and keeping warm, while we was prowling around that frozen wilderness like a couple of lost souls, doing no good whatever, because some damn fool in Helena thought they was killing our cattle. They had more sense.

We didn't even see any game except a few antelope. The weather was still thirty below zero. It's a wonder we wasn't lost; we couldn't see the landmarks half the time on account of what they call ground blizzards in this country, where you couldn't see twenty feet ahead of you because the wind was blowing the loose snow, and yet overhead the sky would be shining. Coming back from Milk River, we was heading for a narrow gap in the hills, a sort of a box canyon on the northwest side of the Little Rocky Mountains, and we couldn't find it, so I gave Grant his head and he got us in there finally. For two days before that we had been traveling across a burnt prairie where there was nothing for the horses to eat, not even when you scraped the ground bare, and that night for the first time I saw horses eat pine tops, they were so hungry.

Sometimes we would get into a coulee where the snow was deeper than we thought, and the saddle horses would make it all right, but the pack horse, being heavy loaded, would bog down and we'd have to shovel him out. To make camp, we always tried to get where there wasn't a drift, and then we would go in under the brush as far as we could, and scoop away the snow to make a place for our beds. If there was any bull pines we'd cut a lot of those and strew them on the ground to make our beds down. But most of the time we was down on the prairie and there wasn't any bull pines.

We built sagebrush fires, and Pike would lay a second

fire for morning, right beside the bed, and throw a saddle blanket over it to keep it dry; when morning come, he would just reach over and jerk off the saddle blanket, and touch a match to one of those fat pine splinters he carried; then we would pull on our overshoes and be dressed. We kept up that life all winter, and Pike thought it was all right, but what bothered me was to be exposing ourselves and punishing ourselves like that when there wasn't no need for it. Going toward Milk River that time, there was one night we couldn't find a sheltered place to camp, because the air was white and the coulees was drifted full, and a cougar ran in ahead of us and showed us where the coulee was. We followed him and we hadn't gone fifty feet when we struck the willows. If it hadn't been for that cougar we'd have froze to death.

In the middle of the winter we went down to Rocky Point. We was out of a lot of stuff, especially coal oil that Pike used for starting fires, and we took the sleigh and followed the high places. We left Pike's ranch at daybreak, and it was ten o'clock at night when we come over the bluffs—eighteen miles in a more or less straight line, which we didn't follow. We got to the edge of the bluffs where the road went down into a drift twenty feet deep, and I went ahead on foot to find the road, but old Pike wouldn't wait, and he went charging down, cussing and roaring, onto the river ice, and we got there somehow, and the lights of Rocky Point was shining on the other side.

There was some Indians camped close there, with their squaws, and we had a pretty good time. We stayed there a week, and when we left there February 14, eight other fellows went with us, going to the C K Ranch, and we had twelve bottles of Indian whisky in the crowd. Christ, what a time!—Deep snow and Indian whisky. It was only twelve miles to the ranch, but we didn't make it until after dark, and the coulees were so drifted you couldn't tell where they were at night, and we had to fire off our six-shooters so the man at the ranch would return the fire to signal us in.

At Rocky Point that winter there was a little half-breed fellow, John Moran was his name, who was always bragging about what a "good man" he was. Well, at that he was an awful good tracker, they said he could track an antelope. But he talked so big, I said: "All right, if you're so good, go down and shoot your gun through a hole in the ice and tell the Missouri to run backwards."

And do you know, he done it. He swaggered down there on the river, drunk of course, and shot his gun through a hole and told the river to run backwards. His wife was one of these black-eyed French breeds, a regular spitfire, and she was sure sore at me. She said: "That calfboy, Teddy Blue. He make my husband shoot through ice, try to make Missouri Ri-verre run back-warrd. Damn fool. Take butcher knife, cut gut."

God, how I've laughed at those French breeds. I must have spent hundreds of dollars buying whisky just to get them to talk. They get everything all mixed up. Like old Mose LaTreille telling me about the time he "crossed the Rocky Mon-tanne, by Chris', run away my va-gonne, broke my horses." That old man was with white people over fifty years, and at the end of that time he talked just the same as when I first knew him.

I knew another French breed by the name of Joe Doney; he had a homestead here in this country, near Black Butte. One winter an ex-sheriff here named Sullivan took pneumonia and died and they had a big funeral for him in town. After I came back from the funeral, I was going to Fort Maginnis for the mail when I met Joe. He says: "Hello, Blue, what you know?"

I said: "Sullivan died."

"Sulli-van, she die? What's a matter?"

"He had pneumony."

"Hell, I got no money. I don' die."

That week at Rocky Point wasn't all fun and Indian whisky. There was a bunch of 600 cattle caught in a pocket under the bluffs of the river, and you couldn't get them up the banks through the drifts on that side. In a few weeks they was reduced to 150; the rest of them went down the air holes, that swallowed up, as we estimated, 6,000 of Granville Stuart's cattle that winter. The ice kind of sloped down to the holes. I remember when we was trying to push them back into the hills, there was one poor cow that had slipped through, and she had her head up and was just holding on by her head. We couldn't get her out—our horses weren't shod for the ice—and so we shot her.

When we was moving that last herd of cattle over across the river in November, John R. Smith, who was to be the boss of Granville Stuart's outfit up there, took over an empty cabin that was just across the river from Rocky Point, and he and another fellow stayed there all winter. They was supposed to keep the cattle back in the hills, keep them from drifting down onto the river and into those air holes, while Pike and me rode the upper part of the range. I was with them when they took over the cabin, and I didn't like the looks of the way it was located. It was right down on the flat, and there was a slough between it and the bluffs on the north side that would cut you off from the hills when the water rose in the spring. What is more, I could see the marks where the ice had knocked the bark off way up near the top of those big cottonwood trees. I told them: "If it was me living in this cabin, when the first chinook come you would find Teddy Blue and his bed up on top of the bluffs."

They made all kinds of fun of me. But when the chinook did come, in March, an ice gorge formed below Rocky Point and the river rose thirty feet in twenty minutes. It drowned Billy and Hippy, the two poor little D H S horses, in the barn. The men got up on the roof of the cabin, and it floated off and grounded on a tree, and they got up in the tree. I wasn't there. I stayed out with Pike until late in March.

Spring came at last. The coulees in some places were piled deep with cattle where they had sought shelter and died, and the ones that were left were nothing but skin and bone and so weak they could scarcely stand. That was the story behind Charlie Russell's picture, "The Last of Five Thousand." A friend of his wrote and asked him that spring how his cattle were doing. For answer Charlie painted that picture of a dying cow and sent it to him.

As I told you, the D H S still had quite a lot of cattle on the south side of the Missouri, and in the spring of '87, Granville Stuart sent me repping clear down to the Big Dry, because they counted on a big drift of cattle to the south. I remember they made a big drive on Timber Creek and got just one steer. The captain of the roundup, Charlie Racer, made fun of all the reps—asked them if they didn't want to go into the herd and look 'em over.

Just to show the loss, we had branded by actual count 10,000 D H S calves on the Flatwillow and Maginnis round-up in the spring and fall of '86; this meant, as we estimated, 40,000 cattle. On the spring roundup of '87 not 100 year-lings showed up, and on a rough count there were only 7,000 cattle all told, mostly steers and dry cows, and these were cattle raised on the Montana range. Double-wintered Texas steers in the Big Dry country got through in the best shape of any cattle in the state, but the loss on trail cattle that had just come into the country was 90 per cent. Fully

184

60 per cent of all the cattle in Montana were dead by March 15, 1887; that is why everything on the range dates from that winter.

In July we were working on the Maginnis range, gathering up what cattle there was left to move them across the river. It was hard work, and we weren't getting a thing; we'd ride all morning and maybe only find a couple of weak-kneed, ganted steers, and they was giving us a lot of trouble, because the weaker and poorer cattle are, the harder they are to drive. That country along Box Elder is as flat as the palm of your hand, and no shade. The weather was hot, and the dead cattle stunk in the coulees—you'd come across little bunches of ten or fifteen or twenty of them piled up—pfew! I can smell them yet. There was an old fellow working with us who had some cattle on the range; I don't remember his name. But I'll never forget the way he stopped, with the sweat pouring off his face, looked up at the sun, sober as a judge, and said: "Where the hell was you last January?"

20

My Reform—I Say a Few Words—
True Love and Troubles—A Tenderfoot Nuisance—
A Different Kind of Tenderfoot—
The Roar of the Falls

All through '87 and most of '88 they were moving cattle across the Missouri up onto Milk River. They had them pretty nearly all up there by the end of '88, but they kept sending reps over south of the Missouri for a couple of years more, picking up a few head at a time. It takes a long while to move a big outfit. You can't possibly get them all in one gather.

But I never went back across the river. For one thing I didn't like that country any more. I got my bellyful of it just like I did the Pecos. And besides, *she* was here, at the ranch, and I wouldn't go away from her.

When I got back from across the river after the hard winter, I looked like a buffalo hunter. My clothes were in awful shape. I remember all the buttons were off, and I had whittled wooden pegs to fasten them together. I had seventeen dollars, but that wasn't enough to buy a new outfit. So I drew forty dollars and went up to Maiden. I never got a stitch—blowed it all and came home broke again and as dirty as ever.

Then Granville Stuart told me: "You've got to go to the Big Dry repping, and you've got to have some decent clothes."

My Reform

That meant I would have to have money to buy them, and I asked him: "How do I stand?"

He looked in the books and said: "Your father made a great mistake when he made a cowpuncher out of you. He ought to have made you a financier. If you work till next August, you'll be even with the company."

But he gave me an order on the store and I did work all summer. And I bought a whole new outfit—new pants, new hat, new six-shooter belt, and a pearl-handled six-shooter, and I cut a big swath when I went down to the Big Dry.

That was the spring I reformed. April 27, 1887, as I know from my diary. I was riding with her—it was after that foolishness about the clothes, the time I didn't get them because I drank up the money instead. And she said she wouldn't have anything to do with a fellow who throwed his money away on whisky. I said: "Is that all you've got against me?" She said: "Yes."

So I quit drinking, threw my chewing tobacco away, quit what little gambling I ever done, and started to save money. It was ten years and three days before I ever took another drink, and then it was some rock and rye for a sore throat. I take a little now. But it shows you what a good woman will do for a man. I look back at it now and laugh. I was so damned in love with her that instead of a D H S on a cow I'd see Mary.

I never did take another chew of tobacco, though all the cowpunchers used to chew. I remember one time we were riding and the wind blowed some of it against my white shirt front and she made fun of me. So for her sake I gave that up, too, and got civilized, and for two years I nearly went bugs chewing gum. I was trying to do without cigarettes at the same time, but then after two years she said she guessed cigarettes wouldn't hurt me; and I smoked after that.

Another thing, and this was the most important, from that time I stayed out of fights. I took the chip off my shoulder and kept my hands away from my gun. It wasn't age that give me more sense, though I was twenty-seven years old. After we were engaged, I took things that I wouldn't have took before that from any man on earth. Why? Simply because of the fear of losing her. I was afraid that if I got into a fight, I might kill a man and have to go to jail or leave the country, and I wouldn't run the risk.

For one thing Mary was almost the first decent young girl I had ever known, and she was a revelation to me. I can't remember that I ever spoke to but three good women in all the time after I left my family until I came to the D H S, and they were all older women, or at least they were married. That storekeeper's wife in Forsyth was one, and the other two were Mrs. Alderson and Mrs. Malone. I'd been traveling and moving around all the time, living with men, and I can't say I ever went out of my way to seek the company of respectable ladies. We didn't consider we were fit to associate with them on account of the company we kept. We didn't know how to talk to 'em anyhow. That was what I meant by saying that the cowpunchers was afraid of a decent woman. We were so damned scared for fear that we would do or say something wrong—mention a leg or something like that that would send them up in the air.

Like the time I got in hot water with that storekeeper's wife in Forsyth, all because I mentioned dining-room girls in her high and mighty presence. It was after the time I'd been taking care of that sick boy in Miles City, and I was telling about how good all the people in the hotel were to us, and I said even the dining-room girls offered to give anything they had to help. I thought this woman acted kind of snippy at the time, and afterwards somebody came to me and said: "Say, you got in a jack pot with Mrs. S. Don't you know any better than to speak of waiter girls in a respectable house?"

Lord, Jesus, that made me mad. As though waiter girls couldn't be just as decent as anybody else. If they wasn't, they wouldn't be working for a living.

Well, that was the kind of thing that could happen to you when you mixed in the company of nice ladies; not all, of course, but some of them; you never knew when they were going to take some little thing you said, meaning no harm, and twist it into a cause for offense. Now that I think back a little more, I did meet a couple of ladies at different times at the N Bar outfit on Powder River. One was the foreman's wife, and the other was the wife of the general manager. The manager's wife was the kind that put on an awful lot of agony, which was also the kind that cowpunchers never could get along with. She thought she was too good for ranch life and everybody connected with it. But the foreman's wife was altogether different. She was a young, smiling, good-natured woman who treated everybody nice —and the whole outfit was in love with her.

It seems almost laughable now to think of the way we stood in awe of a good woman. A group of men would be standing in front of a saloon in the morning—they'd spent the night in town, and they'd be talking about their mashes, and how they'd met a schoolteacher and were going to haze her to a dance, and all that kind of stuff—and you'd see a couple of decent ladies coming down the street and those brave men would just melt away. Didn't want them to know that they patronized saloons.

Well, it was the way we were raised. If you mentioned a decent woman's name in a saloon or a sporting house in those days, you were liable to get your eye shot out. And now if you go in a saloon, there they all are.

I was frightened enough of Mary—just scared to death of her—but not in the same way as these other women I have been talking about. She was the sweetest, dearest little girl I had ever known or thought about, with such a sweet disposition that I knew she could never find fault or act in any way mean. And she never has in all these years. But I thought I wasn't good enough for her and of course that made me fall all the harder.

I worked hard all summer, but I was home at the D H S for a week in August, and while I was there I got a promise. August 7, 1887. I took them all berrying one day in the spring wagon, Mrs. Stuart and the girls. And Mary and I sneaked around till we finally got off by ourselves, and we picked a bucket of raspberries and then we sat down in the shade. And I said a few things and she said a few things, and then it was all settled as far as the two of us were concerned.

But my troubles weren't over, oh, no. They were just beginning. There was a lot of opposition in the family to our marrying, and the biggest part of it came from Mrs. Stuart. Being an Indian, she kept to herself when strangers was around, and she wouldn't sit at the table with them or have much to say, but she was a power in that family. And although she caused Mary and me a lot of grief, I had to admire her just the same because she made a wonderful wife and mother, and no white woman could have raised those girls any better than she did or more in keeping with a white man's ideas. But then she was raised white anyway. Her sister was married to a white man in Deer Lodge, in the mining country, and she was raised up in that family and Granville Stuart married her out of it when she was fifteen.

My Reform

She was dead set against me marrying Mary because she thought I ought to marry Katie, the oldest sister. There was no reason for it, because Katie wasn't in love with me; in fact she had another fellow she was thinking about at that time. But Mrs. Stuart wanted the oldest daughter to be married first; there was a lot of family fuss, and the way things turned out Mary and I had to wait two years.

That was the summer Dick Stuart and I had a tenderfoot riding with us, and before we'd had him very long, we never wanted to set eyes on another one. After that week I stayed at the D H S, Dick and I were sent to Billings to receive a carload of little bulls, then take them up north, and turn them loose among the cattle to replace the ones that were lost during the hard winter. We had Marmaduke along on this trip. Marmaduke was not his real name, but it ought to have been, and anyway it was what we called him. He was the son of a prominent New York clergyman who knew one of Mr. Stuart's partners in Helena.

Rich men's sons from the East were nothing new as far as I was concerned. The range in the eighties was as full of them as a dog's hair of fleas, and some of them were good fellows and some were damn fools. Quite a few, like Teddy Roosevelt and Oliver Wallop, who got to be Earl of Portsmouth later, made good hands and everybody liked them. But this Marmaduke was the most helpless man I ever saw; he had no manners at all around camp, he was just a damn nuisance from start to finish. I remember one time he was supposed to be helping Dick with the pack horse and he tied the knots wrong, and we lost the meat. Well, I wouldn't hold that against him. But that night when we started to unpack, we missed it, and I went back with him almost to where we broke camp in the morning before we found it.

Then a storm come up, and it was late and we couldn't find camp. I fired off three shots with my six-shooter, hoping Dick would answer, and Marmaduke, he was the kind that was always asking questions because he didn't know how to use his eyes and ears and he didn't have any brains, he piped up: "What are you firing at?"

I says: "I'm just taking a couple of shots at God Almighty."

He says: "Oh, please don't say that. I'd rather you'd shoot me than hear you blaspheme."

He couldn't even ride to Black Butte. Now Black Butte is a great big lone mountain that sticks up out of the prairie so you can see it for miles around, and it doesn't take no Jim Bridger or Buffalo Bill to find it. I forgot to mention that along with our other troubles on this trip we turned the bulls loose first on our own home range, which was just exactly where we was told to turn them loose, but it seems that was all a mistake, we should have taken them up to the Missouri. So we had to gather them all over again. We were still gathering them, and we had got a little way north of the D H S bull ranch[1] at the foot of Black Butte, when we run out of flour. So we told Marmaduke to get on his horse and go back to the cook at the bull ranch and get some. He didn't have anything to do only look after gentle horses and the bulls we'd already gathered, while we were rounding them up. I told him how to get there. I said: "You ride straight for Black Butte, and there'll be a half-breed trail right at the foot of it and you follow that to the bull ranch."

He started out in the morning, and at five o'clock he was back at camp and no flour. He said: "Ted, I can't go to Black Butte. I just can't go to it."

1 Where the herd bulls were wintered.

192

Mrs. Teddy Blue, about 1889, when she married Teddy

Teddy Blue in the late 1930's

I said: "What's the matter?"

He said: "I don't know. I can't go to it. It keeps getting further away."

I caught up a horse and I started out then, five o'clock, and I rode to the bull ranch, twenty-five miles, and got the flour, and I borrowed another horse from the foreman and got back at 1:00 P.M., because I had to stand herd. Fifty miles in five hours, because of Marmaduke.

I never could make anything out of a man like that.

Maybe you think we were hard on the poor little fellow and hazed him the way cowboys do to tenderfeet in these Western stories. We didn't, or not exactly. We never give him a mean horse to ride or anything like that. Of course, he just rode the one gentle horse, so we didn't have much chance. But I don't believe we'd have done it anyway. I can truly say that's something I never was in on—giving a bucking horse to a fellow that couldn't ride very good. It used to be done all right, and plenty. They never stopped to think that the fellow might be crippled up. They just figured that they was there to pick him up, so it was all right, and then, too, so many of them had been dumped off themselves without being hurt.

But as for Marmaduke, we didn't like him and we didn't try, and we jobbed him every chance we got. Like a couple of nights after that Black Butte business, we found a lot of moccasin tracks around a little water hole where we camped, and we was talking about what Indians made them, and Marmaduke listened with his eyes just popping.

"What are you going to do?" he says.

"*Do?*" we says: "Why, we'll have to guard these horses." And we stuck him out there in the sagebrush with a six-gun in his hand and told him to stay there all night, and he stayed, scared half to death. After he got back home, we heard he said that it was "literally hell" in the West.

Just to show you what different types there could be, coming up the trail in '83, we had an Englishman with us, by the name of Bigg. He was a kind of a guest of the outfit, on account of his titled connections and so on, and I was supposed to look after him going up the trail, but he never needed no looking after. He had one of these eyeglasses with no string, and he could ride a bucking horse and never lose it. He was quite an all-round fellow, too, because I remember at North Platte, Buffalo Bill's daughters were putting on a show, the *Pirates of Penzance,* it was, and this fellow got up on the stage and sang and made quite a hit. He hung around Miles City for quite awhile, but I don't know what become of him after that. I guess he went back to England.

Taking those little bulls to Milk River was the last work I did for the D H S. After I got through with that I went to work for the Bar 72, on the Moccasin roundup, and when the beef was gathered, we took them to Helena. The night before we had to cross the Missouri River at Great Falls was the night the first train came into Great Falls, and they were having a big celebration and shooting off a lot of fireworks. Pretty soon the fellow on herd—there was only one, because it was a small herd—he come into camp and said: "The cattle just went to hell." And they sure had. Those fireworks had set 'em off so we didn't find some of 'em till fifteen miles back, and they were still going at a trot. It taken us two days to gather them, and the second day we got them strung out again, going toward the river. The boss was a Norwegian chap who did not know a damn thing about a beef herd, anyway not the way I had been taught; so when we got them back to the river and a fellow come out to show us the ford, he says to me: "Ted, you are an old trail man, what is the best way to get the herd across?" Think of a boss asking one of the hands that question!

So I told him the way we always done it, which was to drive the horses in the lead; because horses are not so much afraid of the water and the cattle will follow them. "But," I says, "don't let them ever get over a hundred feet in the lead." He says all right.

Well, we throwed the cavy in, but a lot of women and children had come out on the other side of the river to watch us cross, and that spooked the cattle and they got to milling. By the time we got them to take the water the horses were across. I took the right point, the downstream side, but in spite of all I could do, the cattle worked down on me. Only one little piece in the middle of the river was swimming, about twenty feet across, and I was riding Partner, one of the best swimming horses I ever had. But the current in that piece carried us down a hundred feet, and I could hear the roar of the falls.

Cattle as Wild as Buffalo—Near Death in a Night Run—
Roundups All Summer—Mary Cooks Supper for Me—
We Go for a Ride

I was a Montana cowboy now and for a long time since, and
you will notice I had stopped drifting. A whole lot of this
was due to Mary, but it wasn't all due to her. I was satisfied
up here and didn't want to wander any more. Long before
I met her, in the spring of '84, when they made Johnny
Stringfellow trail boss for the F U F, he offered me fifty a
month to go down to Texas and come back with a herd,
and I turned him down. I meant what I said in Texas that
time about never going back in the brush.

In a way the life up north was a whole lot different from
what it was in Texas and on the trail. For one thing the
people behaved different. I do not know why this is so, but
all old-timers who know the West will tell you that they
did not have so many killings and shooting scrapes after they
got up north as they did in Texas. Matt Winters used to say
that the alkali water they drinked up here took it out of
them, and the winters froze out what was left. Well, Matt
ought to know. Old Matt was one of the ones that tamed
down after he come to Montana, so he got to be pretty near
civilized in the end.

But the country up here was not so different. And when
it came to the work on the range you would have the same
old dry drives, storms, stampedes, and other troubles, and

the stampedes up here were just as bad or worse as they ever were on the trail. After cattle had been on the march a certain number of weeks, they got trail broke so you could handle them. But these range cattle were as wild as buffalo.

You'd be rounding them up in the fall and day-herding the beef, night-herding them, too, and they'd run if you'd so much as blow your nose. You couldn't get off your horse unless you rode over the hill, because if they saw a man afoot that would settle it. You might be watering below a cut bank, and some fool would ride up there and show his head over the bank—and away they'd go. When we were gathering the N Bar beef in '84, the cattle was on water at noon, and a fellow shot his six-shooter off at a jack rabbit, and they made the damnedest run I ever saw. Newman said: "There goes $10,000." Which was just about right, because we had 1,000 head in the herd, and after that they would run on water every day.

When we left here with the D H S beef herd in the fall of '85, we had 1,500 fat steers in the herd, and a damned little fool that we called Bud pounded his quirt on his chaps —and they were off. We ran back on them and rounded them up in the hills, and when we had them together again, Perk Burnett, the wagon boss, asked me to help water them. I said I would if he'd keep the rest of the men in camp. So I rode into the herd and talked to old Gus, our lead steer, about what he'd see in Chicago and so forth and so on, and pretty soon I had him stepping along toward water and the rest following, just as nice as you please. You can talk to cattle the way you would to a person. They know what you're saying. Another day, when Gus got fussy, I rode up and called him a pike-eyed son of a gun and a few other pet names, and he dropped his head and looked at me as though he was ashamed.

The only thing to do during a stampede was to ride in the lead of the cattle—not in front, but alongside—and try to head them and get them into a mill, because once they got to milling they would stop running after awhile. And that was the reason for singing or making some kind of a noise when we were riding with a stampede, because if you could hear your partner you knew he was all right, but if you couldn't hear him he might be down. And if that happened, you stopped trying to mill them, and let them run in a straight direction to get away from him.

I have read stories telling how, in trying to turn a herd during a night run, the cowboys would shoot their six-shooters in front of the cattle. That is like a cowboy with a gun on each hip; it is all fiction; it would only make them run harder. No old hand would do it ordinarily. But I did hear of it being done once, during a night run of a herd of Print Olive's on the South Loup River, in Nebraska. They were heading right for a forty-foot cut bank, and that time

the man shot off his gun and he did turn the lead. But as the swing came around, thirty head were knocked over the cut bank and killed. That is the only time I ever knew of shooting in a stampede.

I was in two stampedes that I will never forget. The first was that one where the man was killed on the Blue River in '76. The second was over here on the Maginnis range, in the fall of 1888. We were gathering beef, and were holding eight hundred big steers in the herd. About ten minutes to two one night, just before time to come off guard, my partner and I met, the way you do, circling in opposite directions around the bed ground. I asked him what time it was and he popped a match—them parlor matches had just come out then. I thought he'd have sense enough to pull off from the herd a little ways, but he didn't. It was a stormy night; the cattle were up and milling, and at the flash of the match they were off.

I followed after them, trying to head them, and at first I heard my partner singing. Then after awhile I couldn't hear him, and I wondered if he was down. I was thinking all the time about that man in '76. So I let them go a little while and got them to the top of the hill, and then I tried again to head them by myself, and they run a couple more times and finally they stopped.

Next morning as soon as it was light he showed up in camp. I said: "My God, where was you?" He said: "I got lost. I couldn't find the herd." He couldn't find eight hundred big beeves that was running and shaking the earth so you could hear them a mile away!

I come so damn near being killed that night! After I got them stopped that first time on top of the hill, they started to run again, and they run hard. My horse was getting tired, and he stumbled over a little bank about a foot high, and fell on me. And I lay there, and as the swing of the herd come around, the outside swing, they come so close that one steer struck me on the hand with his foot, where I had it throwed out to protect myself. I carried the mark for years. I broke a couple of ribs too, where the saddle horn went into them.

My side was hurting pretty bad, but I rode into camp next morning, and that day I went on gathering beef as though nothing had happened. Or I tried to. About noon I rode into a ranch house and asked the girl there for a drink of water. But before she could bring it, I fainted and fell off my horse.

If I had been twenty feet further into the herd that night, I and my horse both would have been trampled just like that fellow in '76. Well, it was all in the game, and all cow-punchers knew it when they were riding like that; they all knew that might be their fate with the next jump the horse took. But they didn't quit and didn't hesitate to risk their lives for their outfits. The fellow that quit that night showed lots of sense, but he never got another job with a beef herd.

I will now go back to where I left off at the end of the year '87. Gathering those bulls was the last work I did for the D H S, because I did not like the new foreman. That year I went down to Billings to spend Christmas with a lot of cowmen who were friends of mine, but it wasn't much of a celebration as far as I was concerned, because I wasn't drinking nothing, only beef tea. I was dead in earnest about this reform business, and was now one of the steady boys you read about in books. From Christmas on I spent the winter at the P W Ranch, up the Musselshell from where the town of Roundup is today, and I would ride to the post office every day in hopes of getting a letter. I got one pretty often. I wouldn't have shown them to anybody in the world, and I couldn't throw them away, so I bought a special wallet to keep them in, and they've been in that old pocketbook, tied up with the same piece of buckskin string, for fifty years. And sometimes now, when Mama goes to town for the day, I get them out and read them over again.

Eighteen eighty-eight was a big year of work for me. I started in March gathering horses for the P W, which was a small cow outfit but a big horse outfit, and in May we got back to their ranch on the Musselshell with 1,200 head. After that begun the regular roundups, and I repped for the P W all summer. Starting in at the mouth of Buffalo Creek on the Yellowstone, May 15, I rode on six different roundups from the Yellowstone to the Missouri and kept it up till October, working back and forth all over the Montana range.

I was keeping my diary all this time, so I have still got a pretty good idea of what I was doing and thinking about

that summer. Aside from the roundups it was mostly Mary.[1]
I got to see her a couple of times. One night in June I came
off night guard at 2:00 A.M., rode forty-five miles, and got to
the D H S in time to help her with the breakfast dishes. And
I was working here on the Maginnis range in September,
the time I got hurt in that stampede. The ranch house
where I asked for a drink and fainted was just a few miles
below the D H S, and the people there took me in and got
word to Stuarts' about me. Right after dinner here come
Mary and Katie Stuart in a spring wagon to find out about
Teddy Blue. Katie says: "Teddy, Mary would not rest till
we came down to find out how bad you were hurt." Mary
says: "It was just like you to stay with the herd and get

---

1 From the diary:

MAY 6. Conley kicked all night because the tent leaked on his face
some men are never satisfied. This morning I blew the boys up with Black
Powder (he threw some of it on the fire) it created a little commotion.

MAY 10. Rode little Nig, the bad horse today, but did not get throwed
off. On herd this evening it was very cold.

MAY 21. Alkali Creek. R L roundup. It has been raining 3 days, we
have been laying here all the time. This is the most disagreeable roundup
I was ever on. I am sleeping outside and my bed is wet as water can make
it but it will get dry sometime. I hope my girl don't have to go out this wet
weather, get her pretty feet wet. (Postscript, December 30) But she did have
to milk in all that wet weather which speaks well for the manhood of the
men on the ranch, damn their lazy souls.

MAY 29 .Throwed the Musselshell cattle on north side of the river. Had
a big dinner at R L ranch. Eggs. Heap washtay.

MAY 30. The boys killed a very large bear today they roped it.

JUNE 6. It was very cold last night this morning it snowed for about 3
hours. How is that for summer?

JUNE 8. Rode Partner to the D H S ranch in 5 hours. It is about forty-
five miles, quite a ride, but I was well repaid at the end of it. Well I should
smile I was. She is about the truck. I caught on to most all the news. She
is sure enough a Daisy Dipped in Dew.

JUNE 12. This is the hardest day's work I ever done on a roundup. I rode
5 horses down to a whisper got into the saddle at 3 A.M. and quit her at
9:15 P.M. to bed slept until 2 o'clock then I went out on night guard till
breakfast. It's hell but it's for Diamond M, and don't you forget it.

We Go for a Ride

killed," and she gave me a kiss, and tears were in her eyes.

I rode with them in the wagon about two miles and led my horse, and then I bid them good-bye and went back to the herd. I told Mary the next stampede I would be the one to get lost, but she would not believe me. That night was my last on herd anyway, as they pulled out for the railroad next day, and I went on to another roundup.[2]

After working all summer for the P W, I finally started for home in October with sixteen horses and twenty-five head of cattle belonging to the Musselshell roundup, including the Dude E and the P W horses and cattle. I had to take them alone over the Judith Mountains, and believe me it was some job. The cattle got tired, and they were getting into the brush all the time, and you couldn't drive them out of it. I just had hell with them. So after it got dark I left them up on the mountain and came down to Mary at the ranch and got her to cook supper for me. They were all in bed but her, and she wouldn't let on that she'd waited up for me, but she heard me coming all right. I had a bell on my horse, and I come down that mountain on a dead run, and it was ringing and ringing.

Next day I got her brother to help me bring the cattle down, and that afternoon I took Mary for a ride. Katie and her mother made an awful row when we got back; they said if Father was here, you'd never have got away from the house, and so on and so forth, up and down and back and forth, till you'd think we'd broke all the Ten Command-

[2] Early in September, according to the diary, he had paid another visit to Mary and had had his troubles with her family, as revealed by the following entry, in a large, angry-looking hand:

"SEPT. 2. Must not talk when there is music must not wear a white shirt without a collar must not say *wy* but why must not write in company WONDER IF I CAN LOVE MY GIRL?"

ments. Mary stood right up to them, and in the end she threatened to walk out. She came to me and said: "Take me out of here now."

What could I do? I didn't have enough money saved to have a home of my own yet, and I couldn't have kept a job, because there wasn't any for married cowpunchers. But I said: "Here, honey, you go to bed and sleep over this, and if you still feel the same way in the morning, we'll go over to Lewistown and get married."

Well, in the morning she was all over it and as sensible as ever, and she said she'd stay.

We didn't know when we was having the fuss that her mother had only three weeks to live. She had another baby the week after all this happened, and two weeks later she died of fever. After I heard the news, I was in too much trouble to ride, from worrying over Mary. So I packed my bed on Billy and came up here once more.

22

I Go to Work in a Mine—
Saving Money Uphill Work—I Hire as Bullion Guard—
Married at Last—End of the Open Range—
Concerning Six-shooters—A Prehistoric Race

We were going to get married six months after Mrs. Stuart's death. But the next spring Mary's sister Katie died of consumption, and so we had to wait again. All during the winter before that, '88–'89, I worked up at the Spotted Horse Mine at Maiden and seen very little of Mary. But one good thing was that we had the old man on our side by that time, and we even got him to carrying letters for us. She had showed him a letter I wrote, when I told her I was going to marry her if I had to hold her with one hand and my six-shooter in the other. She told me he said: "Hmph! If the damned fool feels that way, you might as well marry him."

I took that job in the mine because I was bound and determined that for once I was going to get ahead and save money. It shows you again what the love of a good woman will do for a man. I had never saved a dime or owned any cattle in Montana until I was engaged. I had always blowed my money as fast as I made it or a lot faster, but now I made up my mind to get enough for a start in life and a nice little home of our own.[1] So in December I got a job pushing car

[1] There is pathos connected with this, as revealed by more entries in the diary:

JAN. 1, 1889. I will try and see how little I can spend this year and how much I can save.

down underground. That was the first I ever done that kind of work, and I didn't like it. The powder gave me a headache. I lived in the Spotted Horse boarding house, and I didn't like that either.[2] But it was all for Mary. After I had pushed car for a couple of months, I got to be night watchman at the mill, and that was better, because I drawed the same wages I had always drawed and nothing to do but watch that mill in the night. And all·this time I was going to the railroad with the bullion every month as a bullion guard, fifty dollars for me and my horse. I kept that up all through the summer of '89, till the mine finally played out.

Granville Stuart was in charge of transporting the bullion to the railroad, and we had from $50,000 to $100,000 in gold bricks every month. There was five roads we could take, two to the Northern Pacific, at Junction and Billings, and three to the Great Northern, at Fort Benton, Big Sandy, and Great Falls. He would never tell which road we were going. He would simply take the lead on Maje, his gray horse, and we would get several miles out on the prairie before we knew it ourselves. That old man had sense. We were strung out in such a way that it would be a hard outfit to hold up. Two men would ride about two hundred yards ahead of the team; there was four men in the buckboard, and two men behind about two hundred yards. It was 125

JAN. 25. Can't think of nothing but a pair of Black Eyes. Wonder what I will do this summer? Punch cows I guess.

JAN. 31. Total $62. I must do better than that in February how money does fly.

Eight months later. It seems I can't save money. Don't know why Still it is better than nothing I am worth about $300. It is damn hard to save but I will keep on trying till I do get there.

2 More pathos:

JAN. 6. I get very lonesome evenings having nothing to read and everyone goes down town but me.

miles to the railroad. We'd leave at 1:00 A.M., stop at a ranch for breakfast, stop again from five o'clock to eleven at night, and sleep on relief—and get it on the train next morning at daybreak. The mounted men had to stay just so far ahead of the buggy and ride on a trot all the time. It was a hard trip.

After about two months of being night watchman I went to hauling cordwood between bullion trips. And while I was doing that, a great big stick of it fell on me and put my foot out of business for ten days, and I went down to the ranch to see her. While I was there, I helped put up hay, and helped Mary with the dishes, and helped her run the washing machine that Mr. Stuart bought her—because she had to do the washing for all that big family and he had to have a white shirt every day.

This was in the summer, and all this time she had been sewing on her wedding dress. Dark red velvet, and they'd ordered the material from Helena. She can wear it yet, because she is just as little as she ever was, and she is going to wear it at our golden wedding anniversary, September 29, 1939. They wanted us to be married at the D H S, but at the last minute she got an independent streak and so we drove over to the town of Alpine, with the Anderson girls and a neighbor, and we were married by a justice of the peace.

And that in a way writes the end to the story of my life on the open range, because from now on I wasn't a cowpuncher any more. I took a homestead, kept milk cows and raised a garden, though I still rode and kept cattle, and the truth is that after I was married, I rode much harder and longer hours than I ever done for forty dollars a month.

But I had always worked for big cow outfits and looked down on settlers, and now I was on the other side of the fence, and finding out how damn hard it was to start out poor and get anywheres. I must say the cow outfits still left here were always good to me. When the roundup came near here, I was always with them for a week to get any of my cattle, and the reps would bring them back wherever they found them. Cowboys as a rule were good to the settlers. I have been on both sides of the fence and know both sides, and they are both good if you are honest about it.

After we were married our first home was a ranch we rented and then bought from a man who had moved to the state of Washington. It had a poor frame house, too cold to winter in, and I will never forget our first night on that ranch. It was October 6 when we started to move in, and we only had my cowpuncher's bed laid on the floor, while Mary always had had a nice bed at home and plenty of everything. The pack rats ran over us, and the little girl sure hugged up tight. The next morning we built a fire outside and cooked our breakfast. Granville Stuart had give her all the furniture in her room and we moved that in later; we still have some of it. And I bought a cook stove and a bill of grub from the storekeeper at Fort Maginnis. Then we started to build a log cabin to winter in. I had never cut down a tree in my life, but I flew at it and we got it up. It had a dirt roof and dirt floor but it was warm, and Mary never made a kick.

The next spring I got a small bunch of cattle on shares, and I put in a small crop and a big garden and lots of potatoes. In July, Mary went over to stay with the Andersons to have our first baby, born July 25, 1890. Every night for ten days I rode over to see her. It was ten miles, making a twenty-mile ride after a hard day's work; and I had to milk two cows, work all I could on the garden, tend the water, and ride to hold my cattle close to home.

Saving Money Uphill Work

That fall I beat out oats with a flail on my bed tarp and Mary fanned them out with a milk pan. We sold 1,000 pounds for thirty dollars. I also sold potatoes and butter and garden truck to the coal miners in the mountains, so with my calf increase we made $680 that year.

The next year I got another bunch of cattle on shares, and there were ten good milk cows in the bunch. I got the contract to furnish milk to the Spotted Horse boarding house in Maiden, five gallons a day at twenty cents a gallon. I would get up at four in the morning, milk the cows, drive up to the mine seven miles and back for dinner; then ride after cattle till night. After the garden come on and I got to sell vegetables and butter to miners that lived with their families at the mine, I done a lot better. So when I quit the second Christmas I had made, calves included, $700.

Well, that was the way it went. We got a little better off year by year in spite of hell and sheep. By 1900 we were shipping a carload of beef every year. I built up a good-sized ranch, had over two thousand acres at one time, and in 1919 I was $50,000 to the good. You know what happened when that boom bust. I lost most everything. Such is life in the Far West.

Mary and I raised eight children, five boys and three girls. Six of them are married and doing well; we have fourteen grandchildren and one great-granddaughter.

I did not mention that in 1892 I had filed on a homestead joining our ranch, and had fenced a good-sized pasture on it to winter the poor cattle. You see the range was changing very fast. Fences and sheep and settlers were coming in, and the old-time big cow outfits was going out, and nothing was like it used to be any more. About the time I married and settled down was also about when the old-time range cattle business began to go out of the picture, while fenced pastures and winter feeding and all these modern methods began to look bigger and bigger.

And there was other changes. Along about the nineties a lot of people out here began to quiet down and start leaving off their guns. The country was getting so thickly settled then and the houses was so close together they figured they didn't need them any more.

But I wouldn't give mine up. A six-shooter's an awful lot of company. Suppose you break your leg, you can signal. If you're caught afoot, you can shoot a jack rabbit. If you're held up, you can defend yourself.

And then, too, six-shooters were a great thing for keeping the peace. You wouldn't have any of this calling names and brawling and fighting, where every man was wearing a deadly weapon in plain sight. And as for that expression about a son of a b., I never heard it said with a smile, as they say, before the nineties. In the early days men were soft-spoken and respectful to each other, because it didn't pay to be anything else. It's not like that now. But we were a prehistoric race. We were way behind.

23

Some More about Cowboys—
Independence and Pride—Loyalty to Their Outfits—
Gun Fights—
How Outlaws Were Made

I always carried a gun because it was the only way I knew
how to fight. As Pier La Grange used to say, "If God Almighty'd wanted me to fight like a dog, he'd have given me
long teeth and claws." That was the feeling among the cowpunchers. They didn't know how to fight with their fists.
The way they looked at it, fist fighting was nigger stuff anyhow and a white man wouldn't stoop to it.

You see while cowpunchers were common men without
education, they set themselves away up above other people
who the chances are were no more common and uneducated
than themselves. To show what I mean, Johnny Stringfellow
had a brother Al who was a top cowhand himself—and he's
living yet, in Lewiston, Montana—but they fell out, as
brothers will. Al was working for the Paxton outfit when
Johnny was running it, and he was younger anyway, and
he claims that Johnny was hard on him—would put him
on herd out of turn, and when there was a chance to go to
town he'd send him hunting horses. So Al quit, and just
to spite Johnny he went to work on the section tamping
railroad ties, because a job on the section was considered
the lowest kind of work there was and punching cows was
the highest. As Johnny said, "It's a good thing there wasn't

any sheep in the country or he'd have went to herding sheep."

Another thing about cowpunchers, they were the most independent people on earth. That was why certain customs were followed on the range that you wouldn't find with any other class of men who worked for wages. For example, once a string of horses had been turned over to you, no one, not even the boss, could ride one of them without your permission, though they were his horses. I remember when Con Kohrs, the big, long-legged old Dutchman who was president of the D H S company after the hard winter, came up to the ranch one time and asked the foreman to get him a horse. And the first man the foreman went to said: "Hell no, he can't ride none of my horses." That fellow wasn't aiming to disoblige anybody; he just didn't like to have anybody else riding his horses. Once when Bill Burnett was foreman at the D H S, he came near quitting because Granville Stuart sold a horse out of his string. He asked for his time, but it was just a misunderstanding and was straightened out.[1] Those things were a matter of etiquette, and as I told you, Granville Stuart didn't know a whole lot about the cattle business when he started. If he had gone to the man first and said: "I've got a chance to get a good price for that horse," the man would have said go ahead.

But if they were independent, they were proud too, and that independence and that pride made for the best results in a cow outfit. To tell the truth, it wasn't thinking about the owners' money that made them so anxious to turn out their herd in good shape. What they cared about was the

---

[1] Mr. John R. Barrows, of San Diego, who used to work for the D H S, told me the same story. Said he: "Mr. Stuart evidently wasn't aware of how touchy Texans were about their horses."

criticism of other cowpunchers. They didn't want to hear it said, "That's a hell of an outfit"—so they made it a point to prove the opposite. But that sensitiveness on their part and that belief that their outfit was the best on earth was all to the advantage of the owners, and that was why John Clay was such a fool when he made that speech before the feeders' convention in Illinois, in 1914, attacking the old-time cowpunchers.

"The chief obstacle of the range at that time," he said, "was the cowboys, who were mostly illiterate, uncivilized; who drank and thieved and misbranded cattle, and with a kind of rough loyalty, never told on one another in their crimes."

John Clay[2] was a hard-fisted, money-loving Scotchman who had no understanding of the kind of men who worked on the range. "A kind of rough loyalty" to each other—yes, they had that, in money matters, too. A real cow outfit had only one pocketbook. I've seen them come off herd, when one man had only forty or fifty dollars, and the others would lend him a hundred dollars to go to town. He'd pay it back sooner or later. They were all like a bunch of brothers. And if they weren't, they were no use as an outfit and the boss would get rid of them.

And talking about a cowpuncher's loyalty to his outfit and its owners, that loyalty was one reason there were fights. You might cut a cow and calf out of the herd and I might claim them, and that's where trouble would start. For instance, one time on the roundup a cow was branded with a Lazy Z, which was one of the brands I was repping for, and somebody had put it almost straight up and down so it looked like a Seven L, which belonged to one of the other

2 Founder of the Chicago commission house of Clay, Robinson and Company. For a long time he managed large cattle interests in Wyoming.

outfits. It was a Lazy Z all right, as we finally told from the other marks, but I could have gotten into a fight right there. The cow and calf didn't belong to me, but I'd have been willing to kill and be killed before I gave them up, and where would you find other hands that would do that?

I would like to say more about this business of gun fights, because so much has been written about it in fiction, and it is nearly all exaggeration as far as this part of the country is concerned. I worked up here from 1883 on and I saw a lot of hard work on the range but very little shooting. In fact, from '85 on, until it quit being a range, there was never but one shooting scrape here in the Maginnis district, and then nobody got killed; and over on the Judith and the Moccasin, which were the next ranges, they never had one.

The way trouble started, when it did start, somebody would make a remark about a friend, or a row would come up over riding-horses or some other damn fool ignorant thing, and somebody would take up a thing that wasn't meant and get insulted. They were just young fellows. There was no harm in them, only hot temper. You know how boys are today—"I dare you"—"I double-dare you." Well, it's the same principle as those young fellows getting out there shooting at each other. That was the thing that got many a man, that foolish sensitiveness about personal courage.

I never knew many bad men—oh, I knowed a few, in the seventies. But I can tell you how a fellow that wasn't bad, only unlucky, got to be branded killer and died with another man's knife in him. He was a Texan and his name was George Hay.[3] To begin with he killed a sheriff in the Nations, about 1884. Hay was with a girl one night and the sheriff was stuck on this girl, and he came to the door and

[3] Fictitious.

said: "Let me in or I'll kick the door in." George Hay said: "If you do I'll shoot you." And the sheriff went ahead and kicked it in, and George shot him and killed him. If he hadn't, the sheriff would have killed him, sure.

Now Hay was related to the Dwyers,[4] who had a big outfit in the Nations, and he was with a Dwyer trail herd when this happened. Him and Ira Dwyer, the son, were cousins, and they looked just alike. They were each a quarter Cherokee Indian, they had straight black hair and good features, they were tall, slender, well-made men. After he killed the sheriff, George ran down to where his cousin was at a dance. Ira was wearing a black broadcloth scissortail coat, and the two of them changed clothes, George riding north slow and easy in his cousin's scissortail coat as though he was Ira Dwyer going home from the dance, while Ira put on George's clothes and went south through Texas as hard as he could ride. Of course the Rangers took after Ira, but when they found out who he was they had to let him go.

Meanwhile Hay was riding nights and hiding out in the daytime, and the coat was getting kind of ragged. When he got up on Powder River where the Dwyers had another outfit, he got a fresh horse and a new suit of clothes. Then he rode on down Powder River, going from one Texas outfit to another, till he came to the N Bar, and they gave him a job.

There were plenty of men traveled from Texas up north for the same reason Hay did. Montana was full of them. They changed their names when they got up here, but except for jumping when somebody come up behind them, the first few years, they went along just like everybody else and never had no more trouble.

But luck was against George Hay. Because after he got up to Montana he was accused of a crime that another fellow

4 Also fictitious.

had committed. That fall after the beef roundup started he was alone at the N Bar ranch with Johnny Burgess and one other man. Burgess was waiting for the money to pay expenses on the roundup, and the boss drove out from town with it one day, $500 in big bills, and Burgess put it in the pocket of his shirt and went outside to get some hay for the horses. When he got back, he missed the money—it must have fell out of the pocket when he leaned over. He looked all over the ground for it and couldn't find it. Then he said: "There's only three of us here, and one of you fellows has got it."

The other man, whose name was Jones,[5] got insulted and quit. Hay stayed. A day or two later Jones came back to the ranch, saying it was to get his chaps, when everybody knowed he didn't have a pair of chaps, and what he had come for was to get the $500, where he had cached it. Soon after that he showed up in Miles City making a big splurge, though he didn't have but a month's wages coming to him when he left the N Bar.

Johnny Burgess knew well enough who the thief was, and of course he kept Hay working for him. But Hay felt terrible about it, because Burgess had been good to him. Late that fall Burgess sent him to Medora, South Dakota, to deliver a herd to the Marquis de Mores, and when he got back he hung around Miles City, drinking, and brooding all the time about how to clear his name. He was a high-strung fellow anyway. One night he met Jones coming out of Turner's Theatre, where I got the name of Blue, and he jumped on him like a wildcat, saying, "If you don't own up, I'll cut your damn throat." Jones laughed at him, and Hay cut him halfway through the jugular vein. I came along there a few minutes later, and the sidewalk looked as though a steer had been butchered.

[5] Fictitious.

More about Cowboys

Hay ran to the ferry afoot—somebody'd offered to bring his horse to him. But the sheriffs had it fixed so that the minute anything happened you couldn't get a horse out of a livery stable, and they caught him at the ferry, and he got five years in the pen. I raffled off several bridles for him, and I went to see him, and for awhile there he was talking as though he'd got religion and was going to reform.

But after he got out of the pen a fellow betrayed him, who he was, and the Rangers came and took him back to stand trial for that other killing in Texas. His relatives, the Dwyers, were influential people and they got him out of that. But he was a marked man by that time. I heard that a year or two later he hired out as a gunman to fight for the cattlemen in the Johnson County war. That was a bad business in many ways, but Hay had got to be desperate then; he didn't care; they had made an outlaw of him. When the cattlemen and the hired Texans were all under arrest for killing two men on Powder River, one of the Texans got killed in a fight in the jail and I heard that it was Hay.

But I was always sorry for him because I figured that he was no worse than a lot of us. It reminded me of a saying I read somewhere: There, but for the grace of God, goes So-and-So. It might have been Teddy Blue. Only, as you know, I never did believe much in the grace of God. The love of Mary was what saved me.

24

I Never Was Really Bad—
Cowboys on a Spree—
"The Little Black Bull Come down the Mountain"—
Ogallala Song—The Yellowstone, the Yellowstone

I was never really bad. I never had a reputation as a bad man, only when I was a kid—oh, I was just stinking to kill somebody when I was a kid, because most all the men I associated with had shot somebody, but as I told you, a kid's the most dangerous thing alive. I never got into any crooked stuff, like so many of them—rustling cattle or robbing trains or anything like that. And whatever I may have done that I have reasons to regret, I can say that I was always on the side of the law.

I carried a chip on my shoulder for years, and I got into my share of fights. But I never got into a fight when I was drinking, only when I was sober and knew what I was doing. Because I was always so happy when I was drinking, I loved everybody and everybody seemed to love me.

You see after I got over that early foolishness I wasn't looking for fights, I was looking for fun, and that I believe was the case with nine-tenths of them. They were wild and reckless, it's true, and to understand that, you would have to know the kind of life they led. They were not like these city fellows with a saloon on every corner. They didn't get to drink very often. They were out there for months on end, on the trail or living in some cow camp, eating bad food, sleeping in wet clothes, going without everything that means life to a man—though that was all they ever talked or thought about—and when they hit the bright lights of some little cow town that looked like gay Paree to them, they just went crazy.

Not that they done much damage, usually. They just shot up in the air and shot out a few lights, and as often as not the boss would pay for it all in the morning. Like one time in Douglas, Wyoming, in '86, when Bill Deaton was bringing a trail herd up here to Montana for T. C. Power, the boys started tearing things to pieces in this little saloon, and they roped the bar and drug it out on the prairie. And Bill gave the fellow $250 next day.

Talking about food, do you know what was the first things a cowpuncher ordered to eat when he got to town? Oysters and celery. And eggs. Those things were what he didn't get and what he was crazy for.

A lot of this shooting you hear about was just crazy high spirits. You'd be standing up to the bar with a pipe in your mouth, and bang! the pieces would fall on the floor. Somebody took a shot at it, but it was all in fun. There was a fellow that used to be around Miles City, by the name of Tom Irvine, who was the best shot I ever saw. One night when they were all in the saloon, Louis King, that deputy I was telling you about, was standing there with a cigar in his mouth, and Tom pulled his six-gun out and shot the end off. Louis never budged. He just stuck his face out a little further and Tom clipped another half inch off the cigar so it was down to a little stub. Still Louis never moved, but only stood there with it held out between his lips as though he was daring Tom to come on and shoot again.

Tom said: "You go to hell," and shoved his gun back in the scabbard.

A lot of the saloon men didn't care much for all the shooting. And in later years it got to be the custom for the fellows to take off their artillery when they came in town. They would leave it at the livery barn with their horse and outfit. But that was after things was getting civilized. In the early days nobody did much about it. Only that fellow Marsh, who run a saloon at Rocky Point, was one who knew how to handle cowpunchers. He used to tell them: "Anything goes, boys, but me and the mirror." And he'd put a wineglass out on the end of the bar and say: "I'll bet you the drinks you can't hit it." Of course that took all the fun out of it, and there was never much shooting in his place. The other fellow at Rocky Point would flutter his hands and say: "Don't shoot in here, boys. Please don't shoot." And they made his place a pepperbox.

Another thing about cowpunchers, they didn't have any radio or other forms of entertainment, and they got a big kick out of little things. That was why I got such a reputation among them for singing and storytelling and all that foolishness. It might be a rainy night and they would all be humped up around the camp fire, feeling gloomy, and I'd come in and tell some cock and bull story about my bad breaks at theatres or what I'd done or what I was going to do, and in a minute I'd have them all laughing. Veto Cross, who was our boss coming up from the North Platte in '83, used to say I was worth forty dollars a month just to stick around camp. I never could keep still, you understand, I always had to be talking or singing or doing some fool thing.

And that was how that Little Black Bull song came to be well known at one time on the Montana range; that was my favorite song, and I sang it night and day until I got the rest of them started. I worked it up into quite an act. They would all be standing around in some saloon, or they might be in a roundup camp by the fire, and I would start in like I was going to give them a recitation. As well as I can remember it, it went like this:

"The Alamo had fallen. Brave Bob Travis, that drew the deadline with his sword, lay cold in death at the gate. Davy Crockett, with twenty dead Mexicans beside him and his trusted old Betsy in his hand, lay in the quadrangle. Upstairs Colonel Bowie, the mighty fighter from Georgia, had killed eleven with his terrible bowie knife, before crashing down to inevitable destruction like a giant of the forest before the axeman's repeated blows. Thermopylae had its messenger of defeat. The Alamo had none. It had, however, an avenger, and the hour was at hand. Sam Houston had been in retreat before Santa Anna's victorious army. Now he turned at the Buffalo Bayou and advanced towards the enemy. It was high noon, and the Mexicans were in siesta. Just before he ordered the charge, Deaf Smith galloped up and yelled in a voice of thunder: 'Fight for your lives! The bridges are burnt behind you.' The sun had went behind a cloud, and all Texas held its breath.

About this time they were all looking pretty serious, especially the Texas fellows, when:

The lit-tle black bull come down the moun-tain

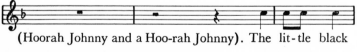

(Hoorah Johnny and a Hoo-rah Johnny). The lit-tle black

bull come down the moun-tain long time a-

go.　A　long　time　a - go.　A　long　time　a - go. And

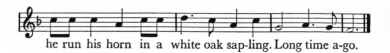

he run his horn　in　a　white oak sap-ling. Long time a-go.

For awhile I had everybody in Miles City singing that song; even the dining-room girls at the hotel were all singing, "Long time ago." I had other favorites, too. "Forty Years a Cowpuncher" was one, and that Laredo song was another—"The Cowboy's Lament," I believe it is usually called. They were singing it when I was punching cows in Nebraska in '76, but I learned "The Little Black Bull" first. That's the oldest song on the range. They say it came out of the Ozark Mountains; and you'll notice it talks about oxen in the second verse. It don't mention steers. I learned it when I was a kid coming up the trail with Sam Bass. They were singing it then, but later they quit singing it.

As for the introduction, that piece of foolishness I used to recite about the Alamo, I made that up. A fellow asked me one time where I got the line about "Thermopylae had its messenger of defeat"—I guess he thought it sounded too educated for a cowpuncher. But I read a few books in my time.

I always had to stop and laugh every time I sang the Laredo song, in spite of it being so sad. Because first he is lying there dead, wrapped up in his blanket, and then he starts in telling this big long story of his life and how he met his downfall.

Cowboy Songs

"I first took to drinking and then to card-playing"—and they'd all be drunk when they was singing it, most likely. Cowboys used to love to sing about people dying; I don't know why. I guess it was because they was so full of life themselves.

"Bury Me not on the Lone Prairie" was another great song for awhile, but it ended up just like a lot of songs on the radio today; they sung it to death. It was a saying on the range that even the horses nickered it and the coyotes howled it; it got so they'd throw you in the creek if you sang it. I first heard it along about '81 or '82, and by '85 it was prohibited.

One reason I believe there was so many songs about cowboys was the custom we had of singing to the cattle on night herd. The singing was supposed to soothe them and it did; I don't know why, unless it was that a sound they was used to would keep them from spooking at other noises. I know that if you wasn't singing, any little sound in the night—it might be just a horse shaking himself—could make them leave the country; but if you were singing, they wouldn't notice it. The two men on guard would circle around with their horses at a walk, if it was a clear night and the cattle was bedded down and quiet, and one man would sing a verse of a song, and his partner on the other side of the herd would sing another verse; and you'd go through a whole song that way, like "Sam Bass." I had a crackerjack of a partner in '79. I'd sing and he'd answer, and we'd keep it up like that for two hours. But he was killed by lightning on Sunday Creek in '85. He was the one who was going to Greenland where the nights were six months long.

After awhile you would run out of songs and start singing anything that came into your head. And that was how a thing like the Ogallaly song[1] got started, that was not really a song, but was just made up as the trail went north by men singing on night guard, with a verse for every river on the trail. That song starts out on the Nueces River, which is the furthest south of all the Texas rivers that flow into the Río Grande, and from there it follows the trail clear on up to the Yellowstone. But when I first heard it, it only went as far as Ogallaly on the South Platte, which is why I called it the Ogallaly song. I must have heard them singing it when I was on the trail in '79 with the Olive Brothers' herd, but the first time I remember was one night in '81, on the Cimarron. There were thirteen herds camped on the Cimarron that night and you could count their fires. A Blocker herd was bedded close to ours; it was bright starlight, and John Henry was riding around the herd singing the Ogallaly song. John Henry was the Blocker's top nigger. I've already told you a little bit about the Blocker outfit, but not enough. John Blocker was the greatest trail man who ever pointed a herd toward the North Star. Ab Blocker was his brother, and he was the fastest driver on the trail.

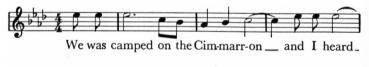
We was camped on the Cim-marr-on __ and I heard_

__ John Hen-ry sing, O - o - o - o - oh,

[1] There is no such thing as an "Ogallala song." The name is pronounced Ogallaly, so Ogallaly it is in this chapter.

I'se gwine north with the Block-er Sev-en herd and Mis-ter

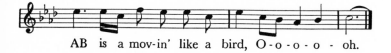

AB is a mov-in' like a bird, O-o-o-o-oh.

Then I heard his part-ner ans-wer him, O-o-o-o-oh, _

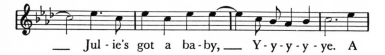

_ Jul-ie's got a ba-by, _ Y-y-y-y-ye. A

lit-tle black-eyed ba-by and don't I love my

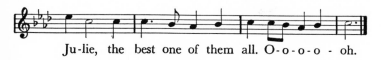

Ju-lie, the best one of them all. O-o-o-o-oh.

I made up those verses after I heard John Henry sing that night, and later I made up a whole lot more of them going north to the Yellowstone, and a lot of fellows in the other outfits were doing the same, making up verses about their own outfits, and the men that worked for them, and their girls. We just sang them any way they come into our heads, they don't look very smooth when you write them down, but they sounded all right. Here is a part of the Ogallaly song as it was sung before I came along and put more to it.

We Pointed Them North

We left Nu-e-ces Riv-er in Ap-ril eight-y

one, with three thou-sand long-horned cat-tle, and

All they knowed was run. O-o-o - o - oh.

We got them through the brush all right,
clear up to San Antone,
We got some grub and headed north,
As slick as any bone.
O-o-o-o-oh.

We crossed the Colorado at Austin, a big town,
And headed north until we struck
The store of high renown.[2]
O-o-o-o-oh.

The old Red River was on the prod
and swum from bank to bank,
We busted her and got across,
A good horse for to thank.
O-o-o-o-oh.

The Washita was running full, but we got them all across
And counted on the other bank,
And never had a loss.
O-o-o-o-oh.

[2] Doan's store on Red River, the "jumping-off place" on the Chisholm Trail.

Then we got to old Dodge City on the Arkansaw
Got a few drinks and some more grub
And pulled out north once more.
    O-o-o-o-oh.

On the Republican we got another storm,
The boss he says this is the damnedest country
I've seen since I was born.
    O-o-o-o-oh.

I never counted the verses—those were only a few—but you could keep on singing it all night. As for the tune, if you could call it that, you know you would get the same tune over and over in the songs we used to sing to the cattle. And there was another song they were always singing on night herd, a sort of croon, about "Lou'siana Lowlands Low-o-o-o-oh." That's all I can remember of it, but it had the same tune as Ogallaly, and so I believe that the Ogallaly song came out of the South originally, like so many other things that went up the trail.

The part I wrote, going up to the Yellowstone, told how we busted the North Platte when she was a mile from bank to bank.

    And pointed north up the old stage road,[3] *O-o-o-o-oh;*
    Crossed the Running Water and down the break-neck hill,
    And then to Gentle Annie's hog ranch on White River.

And a lot more until we come
    Down Punkin Creek to old Tongue River-er-er-er-er,
    And down the flat to old Miles City on the Yallerstone—
    The Yallerstone.

[3] Which ran from Sidney Bridge, Nebraska, to the Black Hills.

227

Then,

> *We busted her—she's cold as hell*
> *O-o-o-o-oh*
> *Mush ice was running down,*
> *O-o-o-o-oh*
>
> *We turned 'em loose on the Musselshell*
> *And that was the end of the Texas trail.*

But it wasn't the end of the Ogallaly song, because after the N Bar outfit went to Miles City, that time in the autumn of '84, I made up a new part to this song, all about Cowboy Annie. I made it up when I was going home with the rest of them, carrying the flag.

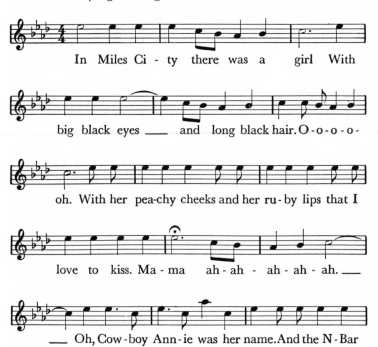

In Miles Ci - ty there was a girl With big black eyes ___ and long black hair. O - o - o - o - oh. With her pea-chy cheeks and her ru - by lips that I love to kiss. Ma - ma ah - ah - ah - ah - ah. ___ ___ Oh, Cow-boy Ann - ie was her name. And the N - Bar

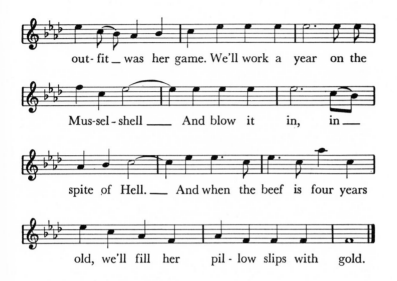

out-fit __ was her game. We'll work a year on the

Mus-sel-shell ____ And blow it in, in __

spite of Hell. __ And when the beef is four years

old, we'll fill her pil-low slips with gold.

Those were the days when every Texas cowpuncher dreamed of getting up to the Yellowstone. And after they had been there and got back to Texas, they might be sitting around the campfire some night and you would hear another fellow ask them: "How far was you ever up no'th?"

"Oh, I been up to the Yellowstone."

"Hell, have you been clear up to the Yellowstone? Christ, I'd like to get up to the Yellowstone. Wonder what chance I've got of gettin' with a Montana herd next season."

You know how it is when you're young—always wanting to get to the place that's furthest. Well, that was the reason they wanted to go to the Yellowstone.

A lot of those Texas cowboys did get up to Wyoming and Montana and settled down like me. They fell in love with the country. A few are alive yet, and I sure love to meet them and talk over old days of fifty and sixty years ago. In 1919, I went up to the Big Stampede at Calgary, Canada, with Charlie Russell, and one day I saw a man who was sizing me up plenty. I says to Charlie: "There is a Texas man." He says: "How do you know?" I says: "See that droop to his shoulders? He got that coming up the trail riding on three joints of his backbone."

So I stepped up to him and says: "Say, old-timer, what part of Texas did you come from?"

He said: "From Mobeetie. How in hell did you know I was from Texas?"

I says: "By that Texas droop to your back. You got that on the long trail." He laughed and said: "I sure did."

I believe I would know an old cowboy in hell with his hidè burnt off. It's the way they stand and walk and talk. There are lots of young fellows punching cows today but they never can take our place, because cowpunching as we knew it is a thing of the past. Riding fence and rounding up pastures ain't anything like the way we used to work cattle in the days of the open range. I will say, though, that there are more good riders now than there used to be, as we always had a bronco buster to take the kinks out of the bad ones, while now every boy in the country wants to ride in these rodeos and they practice all the time. But when it comes to handling cattle, they ain't in it. They are good fellows, but they never will get a show to learn like we did.

A man has got to be at least seventy-five years old to be a real old cowhand. I started young and I am seventy-eight. Only a few of us are left now, and they are scattered from Texas to Canada. The rest have left the wagon and gone ahead across the big divide, looking for a new range. I hope they find good water and plenty of grass. But wherever they are is where I want to go.

Cowboy Songs

FORTY YEARS A COWPUNCHER, *by* Teddy Blue

Come all you wild young cow-punch-ers wher-ev-er you may

be, Come one, come all, come right here now, and lis-ten un-to

me. 'Tis con - cern - ing Lar - ry Wolv - er - ton, a

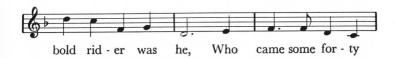

bold rid - er was he, Who came some for - ty

years a - go from Mem - phis Ten - ne - see.

Chorus:

He was for - ty years a cow - punch-er, He

nev - er done things by halves. And his last words on his

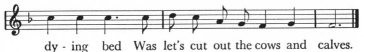

dy - ing bed Was let's cut out the cows and calves.

231

We Pointed Them North

He labored hard for three long years for the SH cow outfit,
And let me say from the very first day they never asked
          him to quit.
He made it his brag that he kept up the drag by the force
          of an old grass rope,
And when they sent him out to relief, old Larry went
          out on a lope.

(Chorus)

In winter time when the hills were clad with snow
On the ranges he did go,
With his big buffalo coat buttoned up to his throat
          all dangers he would dare,
And while the boys were branding the calves,
          old Larry would mark their ears.

(Chorus)

There was one request he did crave,
It's when he died he wanted to ride old Muggins[4]
          to his grave.
Oh lay my spurs upon my breast, my rope and old saddle tree,
And while the boys are lowering me to rest,
          go turn my horses free.

(Chorus)

Give my respects to Bud Burdett,[5] poor Larry he did cry,
And raise me up and let me see old Blue Dog[6] ere I die.
He was so weak he could scarcely speak, in a moment
          he was dead.
Oh let's go in and carve the beef, was the very last
          words he said.

(Chorus)

[4] His pet night horse.
[5] Wagon boss for the S H.
[6] His top cut horse.

Index

Index

University of Oklahoma Press

NORMAN AND LONDON